Essential Soft Skills for Lawyers

What They Are and How to Develop Them

Author
Kim Tasso

Managing director
Sian O'Neill

Essential Soft Skills for Lawyers: What They Are and How to Develop Them
is published by

Globe Law and Business Ltd
3 Mylor Close
Horsell
Woking
Surrey GU21 4DD
United Kingdom
Tel: +44 20 3745 4770
www.globelawandbusiness.com

Essential Soft Skills for Lawyers: What They Are and How to Develop Them

ISBN 9781787423381
EPUB ISBN 9781787423398
Adobe PDF ISBN 9781787423404
Mobi ISBN 9781787423411

Table of contents

Acknowledgements

There are hundreds of lawyers I would like to thank for their time, trust and knowledge. But there are a handful that I particularly appreciate: Kamal Aggarwal, Janice Barber, Jeffrey Greenwood, Bruce Hayter, (the late) Richard Holt, Geoffrey Lander, David Leadercramer and Simon Olswang.

I would also like to thank Sian O'Neill and Lauren Simpson at Globe Law and Business for their perfect blend of professionalism, push and patience.

Many thanks also to the following individuals and firms for their time and thoughts on the contributions and case studies in this report.

Name	Role	Firm
Jo Maude	Project manager	
Helen Peach	Barrister and solicitor	
Jamie Butler	Former director of learning and development	Cleary Gottlieb Steen & Hamilton LLP
Peter Allinson	CEO	Davitt Jones Bould
Geoffrey Lander	Non-executive chairman	Davitt Jones Bould
Janice Barber	Former managing partner	Hempsons
Ben Evans	Founder	Humantalk
Holly Gavaghan	Business development director	Keating Chambers
Mark Day	CEO	Law South
Sara Palmer	L&D manager	Law South
Fiona Jackson	Client adviser	LexisNexis InterAction
Sue Bence	Director of legal services	LexLeyton
Oliver Taylor	Marketing manager	Mundays
Carolann Edwards	Global director of learning and organisational development	Norton Rose Fulbright
Denise Kitchener	Head of business development	Osbornes Law
Alyson Pellowe	Director	People Vision
Ray D'Cruz	Founder/CEO	Performance Leader
Chris Hunter	Head of business development and marketing	rhw solicitors
Julia Robinson	Senior manager, professional development and training	Ropes & Gray
Neil Denny	Solicitor	Roythornes
Sue Colton	Director and founder	SJC Consulting
Victoria Heming	Human resources director	Thomson Snell & Passmore

I. Introduction

The most important single ingredient in the formula of success is knowing how to get along with people.
Theodore Roosevelt[1]

The care economy will favour those people with good interpersonal skills.
Ian Pearson, Futurizon[2]

Let's call them real skills, not soft. Real because even if you've got the vocational skills, you're no help to us without these human skills, the things that we can't write down, or program a computer to do.[3]
Seth Godin

The legal sector continues its love affair with innovation and the potential impact of technologies such as automation, artificial intelligence (AI), machine learning and blockchain. This is primarily focused on enhancing the efficiency of the legal product. Yet futurists are more concerned about futureproofing jobs and careers through the human skills which are not so easily replaced by technology. Ian Pearson once predicted: "People whose only advantage is intellectual will lose out, as will those with no skills at all."[4]

Large and small law firm clients assert that what differentiates the best lawyers are their soft skills: the ability to communicate, to manage relationships, to solve complex problems in innovative ways, to ensure that global teams work together harmoniously and to add value beyond the delivery of first-class legal solutions.

I have spent more than 25 years working with lawyers in the United Kingdom and overseas. Occasionally, I am struck by the chasm between the brilliance of their technical legal skills and the paucity of their soft skills when it comes to developing strong relationships both within and beyond their firms. Good soft skills are required for leadership, team development, change management, business development and service delivery.

The desire to be a 'trusted adviser' still resonates in the legal profession. But that ideal relies on high performance in a range of soft skills; while the training programmes and academies of many law firms remain exclusively or predominantly focused on technical legal skills and technology competencies.

The ambitious aims of this report are as follows:

- to explore the importance of soft skills for lawyers;
- to understand the views of lawyers on soft skills;
- to discover how HR and learning and development (L&D) professionals within leading law firms are promoting the development of soft skills in their lawyers;
- to identify the essential soft skills for modern lawyers;
- to provide some insight into those essential soft skills for lawyers; and
- to signpost relevant sources for further exploration of soft skills for lawyers.

This report is an introduction and overview. Globe Law and Business envisages interest in possible follow-up titles on these topics looking at specific soft skills in more depth.

I am grateful to the lawyers, HR, L&D, business development and psychology professionals who have taken the time to share their views on the essential soft skills for modern lawyers (for further details see the Acknowledgements section).

Welcome to the brave new world of soft skills development for lawyers.

II. What do we mean by 'soft skills'?

A 'skill' is easy to define: "the ability to do something well, usually as a result of experience and training".[5]

And there are many skills. *The European Dictionary of Skills and Competencies* (DISCO)[6] provides a structured vocabulary for the description of skills and competencies in different contexts of the labour market. This comprehensive understanding of skills and competencies includes professional competencies, personal attitudes, values and behavioural patterns, irrespective of whether they have been acquired formally or informally. DISCO consists of about 10,000 terms (about 7,000 preferred terms and 3,000 synonyms) per language for 10 European languages.

But there are differing views about what exactly constitutes soft skills.

1. Technical legal and technology skills

Among lawyers, technical legal skills dominate. Lawyers' initial training and much of their continuing professional development (CPD) (now 'continuing competence') is focused on acquiring in-depth legal knowledge and an advanced understanding of the process of law. Keeping technical legal knowledge up to date is a relentless pressure in today's fast-paced, increasingly global and regulated world.

On top of this, lawyers must continually learn new technology skills – how to deploy the latest practice and case management, client relationship management (CRM) and legal project management (LPM) systems. They must remain alert as to how to guard against cyberattacks and how to use analytics to optimise the online client experience. The coronavirus crisis created a steep technology learning curve for many lawyers as they transitioned to working from home.

Many lawyers work at the bleeding edge of technology to see how process improvement can make the business of law more efficient and error-free, and remove the cost of humans completing repetitive but expensive tasks.

So technical legal skills and technology skills are essential for lawyers. But these are not what we would consider soft skills.

2. Is it practical intelligence?
Psychologist Robert Sternberg[7] considered that there are three forms of intelligence:

- componential (based on academic proficiency);
- experiential (the capacity to be intellectually flexible and innovative); and
- practical (attaining fit to the context).

From this, one might argue that analytical intelligence is aligned to hard skills and practical intelligence to soft skills.

Malcolm Gladwell, in *Outliers: The Story of Success*,[8] says: "You can have lots of analytical intelligence and very little practical intelligence or lots of practical intelligence and not much analytical intelligence."

3. Is it commerciality?
Some define 'commerciality' as the ability to produce a profit. Commercial skills – commercial awareness or business nous – relate to business aptitudes such as strategic thinking, financial awareness, numeracy and a grasp of both macro and micro-economics. For lawyers, it denotes an ability to step out of the narrow focus of the legal process and see the bigger picture – and clients' business aims and challenges – through a commercial lens.

'Business acumen' is "keenness and quickness in understanding and dealing with a business situation (risks and opportunities) in a manner that is likely to lead to a good outcome".[9]

4. Are they emotional or people skills?
So, are soft skills simply those skills which do not qualify as technical or technology skills?

Wiki says: "Soft skills are a combination of people skills, social skills, communication skills, character or personality traits, attitudes, career attributes, social intelligence and emotional intelligence quotients, among others, that enable people to navigate their environment, work well with others, perform well, and achieve their goals with complementing hard skills."[10]

Dale Carnegie's famous self-help book *How to Win Friends and Influence People* was first published in 1938.[11] Some would argue that Carnegie's work, which has sold more than 15 million copies worldwide, is the definitive guide to soft skills.

Thomas W Derry,[12] CEO of the Institute for Supply Management (ISM), used the term 'essential skills' when launching ISM's Mastery Model to describe the many interpersonal attributes required on the journey to achieving accreditation to members of his organisation:

> *Emotional intelligence quotient is the technical term for soft skills. I like this term simply because it contains the word 'emotional', which pretty much sums up what soft skills entail. Calling it a 'quotient', however, raises the argument that EQ, like intelligence quotient (IQ), is something you're born with, and can't be improved upon which isn't true. Our brains are 'plastic' and can be reshaped through experience and learning.*[13]

"Many lawyers work at the bleeding edge of technology to see how process improvement can make the business of law more efficient and error-free, and remove the cost of humans completing repetitive but expensive tasks."

In 2016 another procurement specialist, Hugo Brit, said: "The simplest, and possibly the most accurate alternative for soft skills is 'people skills'. After all, every one of these skills involves dealing with people, while hard skills can generally be put to use sitting alone at your computer".[14]

5. Are they attributes?

Hard skills include specialised knowledge and technical abilities, such as tax or patent law expertise. Soft skills are more about emotions, behaviour and thinking, personal traits and cognitive skills. They are typically more difficult to measure.

I recollect from a conference that a leading City lawyer once said that the four attributes lawyers need to succeed are affability, availability, ability and affordability.

This report explores the views of what constitutes soft skills in the UK legal profession. What are the essential soft skills for lawyers and how can they best be developed for tomorrow's legal practitioners?

"Hard skills include specialised knowledge and technical abilities, such as tax or patent law expertise. Soft skills are more about emotions, behaviour and thinking, personal traits and cognitive skills. They are typically more difficult to measure."

III. The importance of soft skills for lawyers

In 2007, in a report produced with Carnegie Mellon, Stanford Research Institute revealed that in industry and commerce generally, 75% of long-term job success depends on the mastery of soft skills and only 25% on the mastery of technical skills.[15]

But just how important are soft skills for law firm leaders, lawyers and those working in the legal sector? Many studies in recent years, both in the United Kingdom and internationally, have set out to answer this question. Some of these studies are considered below.

1. World Economic Forum's *Future of Work* report

The World Economic Forum's (WEF) 2018 *Future of Work* report,[16] which interviewed global companies employing a total of 15 million people (of whom 1.3 million were in professional services), stated: "Amongst the trending skills in demand are: analytical thinking and innovation, active learning and learning strategies, creativity, technology design and programming, critical thinking and analysis, complex problem-solving, leadership and social influence, emotional intelligence, reasoning and systems analysis."

Citing the WEF's *Future of Jobs*,[17] a 2018 *Forbes* article by Avil Beckford listed the top 10 skills demanded in 2020 as:

- complex problem solving;
- critical thinking;
- creativity;
- people management;
- coordination with others;
- emotional intelligence;
- judgement and decision making;
- service orientation;
- negotiation; and
- cognitive flexibility.

2. Management experts

In 1992 'technical mastery' was identified as the most important competency in a Center for Creative Leadership survey titled *Expanding the Leadership Equation: Developing next generation leaders*.[18] But when the survey was run again in 2012, technical mastery was no longer included among the most important competencies, displaced by soft skills such as self-motivation/discipline, effective communication, learning ability, self-awareness and adaptability/versatility.

A 2015 *Harvard Business Review* article[19] reporting on a PwC survey of 1,322 CEOs in 77 countries mentioned curiosity and open-mindedness as leadership traits that are becoming increasingly critical in challenging times.

A 2018 report by Bersin™ Deloitte[20] noted that employers are as likely to select candidates for their adaptability, culture fit and growth potential as for in-demand technical skills. Employers such as Google, Amazon and Microsoft have highlighted the importance of learnability – curiosity and a thirst for knowledge – as a key indicator of career potential.

In January 2019 a *Harvard Business Review* article[21] reported that in a Manpower Group survey of 2,000 employers, more than 50% of organisations listed problem solving, collaboration, customer service and communication as the most valued skills.

QDooz – a digital CPD provider initially launched in the United Kingdom in 2019, but now paused as a result of the coronavirus pandemic – made the following observations on the importance of soft skills, now and in the future:[22]

- Fifteen million jobs in the United Kingdom that exist today will not exist in 10 years.
- Ninety-two per cent of executives in the United Kingdom rate soft skills development as a critical factor when screening candidates.

- AI, technology and automation are threatening employability.
- Seventy-nine per cent of teachers say that soft skills will be key to helping students in an increasingly unpredictable economy and changing world.
- Soft skills will increasingly become a defining competitive advantage.
- Soft skills can boost your lifetime earnings by up to 14%.

QDooz went on to state: "According to the National Qualities Index (NQI) 49% of business decision-makers think their staff need more soft skills training to be more effective and successful at work."

In research published in January 2020, LinkedIn[23] analysed job advertisements posted on the site and identified the top five soft skills sought as creativity, persuasion, collaboration, adaptability and emotional intelligence (EQ).

In February 2020, LinkedIn[24] reported that 140 top CEOs identified nine critical mind-sets, including being a global citizen, humility, openness and curiosity.

3. Client perspective

We can also consider lawyer soft skills from the client's perspective. In Canada, in 2006, Kara MacKillop and Neil Vidmar found that communication and relationship problems were responsible for 46% of all legal malpractice claims and 51% of claim costs.[25]

In 2017 the Solicitors Regulation Authority (SRA) and the Legal Ombudsman jointly commissioned London Economics and YouGov[26] to conduct independent research into the experiences of people making complaints about solicitors' services. It found that both legal services users and firms report that most complaints relate to delays or failures in communication.

4. Solicitors Regulation Authority

The SRA uses continuing competence to ensure that solicitors can do their jobs to the standards expected of them. The SRA lists four core competencies to focus on, of which three relate to soft skills:

- ethics, professionalism and judgement;
- technical legal practice;
- working with other people; and
- managing yourself and your own work.

An article published in the *Solicitors Journal* in March 2019[27] stated: "The belief that soft skills training is a new phenomenon in legal services is not entirely accurate. It started more than 20 years ago when the LPC course offered training in negotiation, interview techniques and communication."

5. Legal sector commentators

Many years ago David Maister, a leading management expert on law firms, outlined eight dimensions of professional service firm distinction, including special client counselling skills and client listening skills – both of which are heavily reliant on soft skills. It is no surprise that another of Maister's dimensions is training excellence.

In his 2017 book entitled *Soft Skills for the Effective Lawyer*, US legal expert Randall Kiser[28] observed that: "It is soft skills that most frequently distinguish an exceptional attorney from an ordinary attorney." He also quoted law professor Deborah Rhode: "Lawyers lacking in soft skills tend to devalue their importance rather than address their absence." Kiser reported that the most important non-cognitive skills include resilience, self-efficacy, optimism, emotional granularity, feedback elicitation, curiosity, goal achievement, embodied cognition and mindfulness.

A 2018 article published in *The Counsel Network*[29] suggested that the soft skills that set great lawyers apart from the rest include:

- a genuine desire to help other people;
- high personal integrity;
- humility and sensitivity;
- simplicity;
- empathic listening;
- confidence and persistence; and
- discipline, dependability and loyalty.

In a September 2019 article in *Forbes*, Mark A Cohen argued: "Law – like so many industries – is undergoing a tectonic shift. It is morphing from a lawyer dominant, practice-centred, labour-intensive guild to a tech-enabled, process and data-driven, multidisciplinary global industry."[30] He continued: "Legal knowledge is becoming a skill to be leveraged with new competencies." He suggested that there are three main elements of practice – legal expertise, judgement and persuasion – adding: "Lawyers must learn new skills like project management, data analytics, deployment of technology and process design."

In March 2019 industrial psychologist Sonica Mouton[31] said:

> *According to the respected legal futurist, Richard Susskind, it's no longer just enough to teach the old basic skills of lawyering in the new, AI driven, automated economy. A new type of lawyer is needed who is not only trained in the use of coding and legal technology, but also in skills that AI will not be capable of*

> *automating. These include the very 'human' capabilities of creativity, empathy, compassion, and emotional intelligence. More and more if you want to practise law you need to become a trusted adviser to your client, you need the ability to listen, to communicate and relate to others to help solve their legal problems.*

A March 2019 article by Susan Smith Blakely in the *ABA Journal*[32] warned that law firms should not overlook the value of soft skills. She listed the soft skills that are considered most important to the success of young lawyers as follows:

> *1. Being a good communicator in a variety of modes (email, text, phone etc)*
> *2. Being empathic and developing strong emotional intelligence*
> *3. Having a sense of humour and not taking yourself too seriously*
> *4. Finding mentors and sponsors to enhance career development*
> *5. Understanding office politics and procedures*
> *6. Ability to accept feedback and use it positively to improve*
> *7. Networking and developing new work*
> *8. Adaptable to a variety of tasks and work settings*
> *9. Assertive in the desire to learn about the business of law*
> *10. Comfortable with collaboration and team work*
> *11. Creative thinker*
> *12. Leadership and management skills*
> *13. Negotiating skills*

A May 2019 article by Jemma Smith, editor of *Prospects*,[33] argued that the seven skills for a successful law career are as follows:

- commercial awareness;
- people skills;
- communication;
- attention to detail;
- research and analysis;
- creative problem solving; and
- resilience and self-confidence.

In his 2019 book *The Human Edge*,[34] Greg Orme presented convincing evidence that the vast majority of existing jobs will be threatened by AI – both with the current narrow intelligence and with future general and super AI. He reported on a large survey of US employers which revealed that 72% of people were worried about AI. This message has also been regularly repeated by legal commentators Richard and Daniel Susskind.

In his book, Orme argued that we must use human skills – particularly consciousness, curiosity, creativity and collaboration – in response to AI, and predicted that problem-solving skills will become more important. He further observed: "For the first time, creative thinking is on the same playing field as people management, problem-solving and critical thinking."

In September 2019 LexisNexis produced a Bellwether report titled "The Good Solicitor's Skill Set – Is there a disconnect between assumptions and reality?"[35] The report was compiled using data from eight in-depth interviews with solicitors in small firms and small offices of larger firms, as well as online surveys completed by 176 solicitors in England and Wales. The key findings were as follows:

- Nine in 10 solicitors agree that good business skills and good human skills are of increasing importance if solicitors are to be successful.
- Four in five of the attributes identified as the top priorities for success are human skills.
- Of the five attributes identified as a 'top priority' for a good solicitor, four – common sense, inspiring trust, willingness to listen and use of normal language rather than legal jargon – are human skills.
- Only one business skill makes an appearance in the list: developing and retaining clients.
- Four of the top 10 skills lacking in the profession at the moment relate to business: entrepreneurial skills, a good understanding of commerce, a service industry mentality and the ability to generate business.

Table 1 opposite reproduces a table from this report listing the most important attributes for lawyers.

In January 2020 Paul Hodkinson,[36] editor of *Legal Week*, suggested that as a result of the increasing use of technology, lawyers are losing the human touch and the depth of lawyer-client relationships is diminishing.

Most of these comments are aimed at lawyers in private practice. The view is often that in-house lawyers have an advantage, in that their more varied commercial experience means that their soft skills are more finely honed.

6. Commercial and trusted advisers

Lawyers serving commercial clients often look to the commercial adviser model, while those serving private clients orient towards the trusted adviser model. Soft skills are prevalent in both.

Table 1. Importance of attributes to thrive as a solicitor

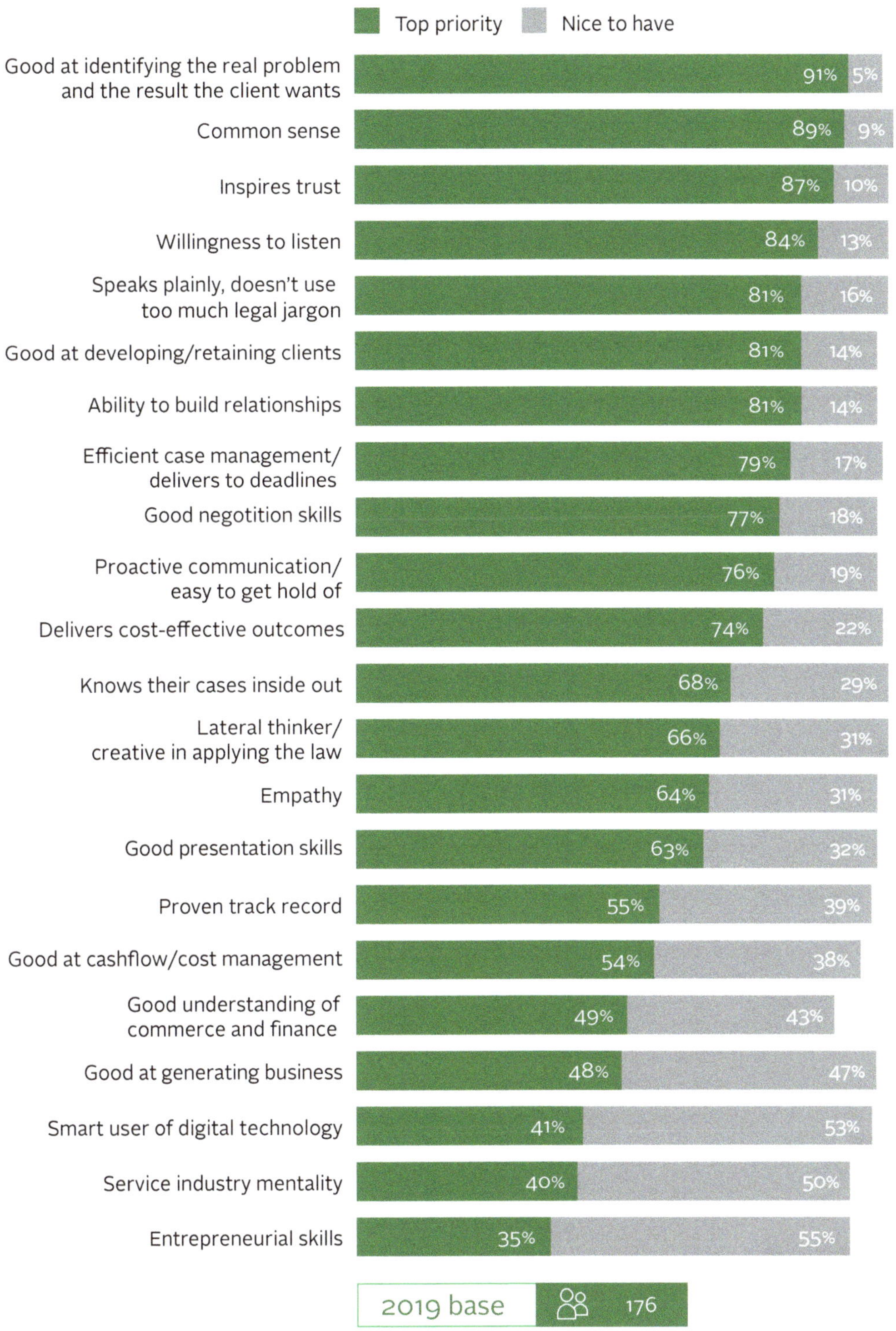

Source: Reproduced by permission of RELX (UK) Limited, trading as LexisNexis.

The seven attributes of a commercial adviser are generally considered to be as follows:

- Understand the client's desired outcomes.
- Understand the client's business.
- Understand the client's economics.
- Understand the client's people.
- Agree the scope.
- Build practical solutions.
- Communicate for impact.

When we consider the trusted adviser model, we see that many of the 10 attributes are reliant on soft skills:

- Focus on the long-term relationship.
- Put clients' interests before your own.
- Be genuinely interested in clients and their businesses.
- Understand clients' underlying wants.
- Be reliable – do what you say you will do.
- Be credible – but don't try too hard.
- Get up close and personal.
- Connect emotionally.
- Be genuinely passionate and enthusiastic.
- Be authentic.

The need for a client-facing and commercial mind-set

Sue Bence is an experienced litigator, having worked at Clyde & Co, Kennedys, Leigh Day and Slater & Gordon (where she held roles in performance improvement and operational efficiency). She has an MBA and is now director of legal services at LexLeyton, a start-up eight-lawyer employment service. This is part of Leyton Group, which is a global privately owned innovation funding consultancy.

> *Having moved from the consumer legal services sector, I underestimated the mind-set challenge of lawyers in the commercial sector. I am building a law firm within a fast-moving, high-energy, super-agile entrepreneurial company with a brilliant, commercially minded sales operation as its core competency. After 30 years as a solicitor, a key challenge for me is to find and recruit lawyers who have the blend of soft skills and qualities that creates an umbrella mind-set that is utterly focused on the client's needs and our role, which is to add value to clients.*
>
> *I need lawyers who see every single conversation as an opportunity to reinforce the relationship and explore how we can add further value. That's a sales mind-set first and foremost.*

"A key element of on-boarding and continuing to support the professional development of lawyers is relevant training, to help lawyers understand that clients want more than an exposition about the law – they want a solution to their challenges and a clear pathway to achieving their goals."

Technical expertise is taken for granted – that's a given; the lawyer's job is to be able to demonstrate in a tangible way that we can add value to the client. To do this, you need to understand the individual client and the context of its business and the challenges it faces. At interview stage, I don't examine people's employment law expertise, but their commercial nous and their client focus.

Our parent company has huge resources for sales training. We invest an extraordinary amount in training. We take our lawyers through a lot of training day in, day out – using various sales methodologies and digital sales prospecting and support tools with sales leadership and support that we are able to access through our group.

We use social learning rather than a traditional form of learning management system – it's a great way to encourage collaborative learning. We use storytelling to show how we helped clients and improved their overall business performance, which in turn enables us to highlight the key value elements of our range of services.

I need lawyers who can bring a real energy and optimism to client conversations – who are natural and who have personal impact and a real passion for what they do. They need to show clients that they are interested and be totally present and engaged during any form of communication. Lawyers shouldn't start each conversation with excuses about why they have been slow to respond – they need the client to feel as if they are the only client we serve. Our lawyers never leave a conversation without agreeing the next steps, the timescales, the costs and the follow-up.

Lawyers need to go beyond creating trust in the relationship – committing to do what they say they will do and when. They need to deliver more than what the client is expecting. We are all consumers and know what it feels like to have a great customer experience on the telephone – as lawyers, we need to provide the same levels of service. Is it something about the internally focused work ethic of lawyers or is it a fundamental arrogance that the technical aspects of the law outweigh everything else?

The range of skills needed by modern lawyers is extraordinary. Everything is important – even something as basic as time management to get everything done within short timescales. For me, a key element of on-boarding and continuing to support the professional development of lawyers is relevant training, to help lawyers understand that clients want more than an exposition about the law – they want a solution to their challenges and a clear pathway to achieving their goals.

7. T-shaped lawyers

The earliest reference to the idea of 'T-shaped people' was by David Guest in 1991[37], although it is reported that McKinsey & Co management consultancy used the term in recruitment during the 1980s. In 2014 law graduate R Amani Smathers[38] presented the idea of the T-shaped lawyer at the ReInvent Law Conference in New York City.

The vertical bar of the T represents the depth of skills and expertise in a single field. The horizontal bar represents the ability to work across disciplines with experts in other areas and to apply knowledge from areas of expertise other than one's own. T-shaped people are comfortable in multidisciplinary roles.

Increasingly, professionals are encouraged to specialise, so they invest considerable time in developing advanced knowledge in their area of expertise. The result is I-shaped people, who have an incredible depth of expertise.

However, to work on strategically significant projects and to be promoted to senior management, there is a need for a broader perspective, with an appreciation of other disciplines such as finance, human resources, operations and technology. This broadening of knowledge and skills – across the horizontal stroke of the T – is often accompanied by enhanced commercial knowledge. It enables people to be more systemic in their thinking: to see the potential impacts on other processes when a change is implemented in a particular area.

T-shaped people have both depth and breadth. This idea is relevant to all professionals, not just solicitors. Other terms to describe the concept include 'generalising specialist', 'technical craftsperson', 'renaissance person' and 'master generalist'.

David Epstein's 2019 book *Range*[39] is a valuable read for those managing the long-term development of lawyers.

There is also interesting material relating to multi-potentiality. This is an educational and psychological term referring to people – particularly those with strong intellectual or artistic curiosity – who have the ability and preference to excel in two or more different fields of life. Multi-potentialities or polymaths have no 'one true calling' the way specialists do. The ability to draw from many different mental models is considered valuable in strategy, creativity and problem solving.

8. O-shaped lawyers

In a video on the Apperio site,[40] Dan Kayne, general counsel (routes) at Network Rail, described what he expected from future in-house lawyers (currently 22% of the profession – around 25,000 solicitors). He stated that in-house counsel must manage the relationship with the internal customer base and know how to buy, implement and embed technology and tools. To do this effectively, they must be well-rounded people with the following attributes:

- openness – an open mind-set that is welcoming to new ideas and an awareness of how they feel (ie, high levels of EQ – see p 27);
- opportunism – the ability to identify and seize opportunities;
- originality – a creative and decisive approach in choosing new ideas; and
- optimism – the ability to see things positively.

Interestingly, these ideas are almost entirely reliant on great soft skills.

9. The Delta Model

In November 2019, in an article in *Legal Evolution* entitled "The Delta Model: simple, accurate, versatile",[41] the authors imagined a world in which law schools, employers and clients all shared a common touchstone for lawyer development. The Delta Model is as follows:

- The law:
  - subject-matter expertise;
  - legal research;
  - legal analysis; and
  - legal writing.

- Business and operations:
  - business fundamentals;
  - project management; and
  - data analytics.

- Personal effectiveness:
  - relationship management;
  - entrepreneurial mind-set;
  - EQ;
  - communication; and
  - character.

Innovation and robot-proof skills

Julia Robinson is senior manager for professional development and training in the London office of Ropes & Gray, which has 1,200 lawyers across 11 offices in the United States, Asia and Europe. She began her legal career at DLA Piper before spending several years as a corporate associate at Covington & Burling in London. She then went into teaching as a senior lecturer and programme leader on the Legal Practice Course (LPC) at BPP.

She has since worked in learning and development at Ashurst and more recently Slaughter and May. It was at Slaughters that she created and delivered its first innovation training programme, which had three elements: digital literacy, creativity and productivity. It also included sessions on coding awareness, digital habits and design thinking.

Following her move to Ropes & Gray, Robinson has taken these ideas to the next level, developing a "Robot Proofing for Lawyers" programme. She was inspired by a *Financial Times* article in which soft skills were reframed as "robot-proof skills".[42]

The programme includes sessions on effective collaboration, critical thinking, design thinking, inclusive communication and trust in virtual teams. The idea is that by focusing on relational skills, lawyers can deepen their relationships with clients and their personal effectiveness, while still taking advantage of technological advances.

IV. Emotional intelligence for lawyers

Many of the soft skills needed by lawyers are enshrined within the scope of EQ, and emotional and social intelligence.

EQ is the capacity to be aware of, control and express one's emotions, and to handle interpersonal relationships judiciously and empathetically. Over the years, research into EQ has suggested the following:

- Tested alongside 33 other important skills, EQ subsumes most of them, including time management, decision making and communication.[43]
- EQ accounts for 58% of performance in all types of jobs, and is the single biggest predictor in the workplace and the strongest driver of leadership and personal excellence.[44]
- Only 36% of people tested can accurately identify their emotions as they happen.[45]
- Ninety per cent of high performers are also high in EQ – people with high EQs make more money (an average $29,000 more per annum in one study).[46]
- Self-management skills appear to increase steadily with age.[47]
- While women and men are roughly equal in their ability to recognise their own emotions, men have recently caught up in their ability to manage their emotions and in other skills – so the gender gap is closing.[48]

- Middle managers have the highest EQ scores in the workforce and CEOs the lowest.[49] Yet researchers have found that EQ skills are more important to job performance than any other leadership skill.
- US executives averaged 15 points lower than Chinese executives in self-management and relationship management.[50]

"Although 95% of people think they're self-aware, only 10–15% actually are."[51]

It was argued in the past that there is a negative correlation between extremely high levels of intelligence quotient (IQ), which measures cognitive skills, and EQ. This presents a potential problem in law firms, where such a high value is placed on intellectual capabilities.

1. What is emotional intelligence?

Although there are several models, Figure 1 sets out the main components of EQ.

Figure 1. Four core emotional intelligence skills

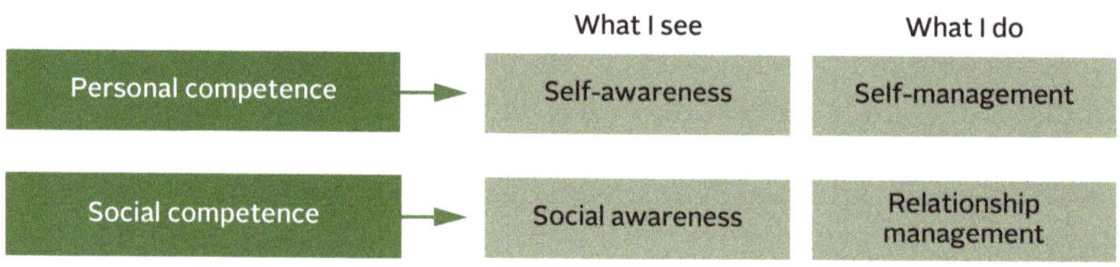

Source: Emotional Intelligence 2.0, Travis Bradberry and Jean Greaves

This figure comes from *Emotional Intelligence 2.0*[52] by Travis Bradberry and Jean Greaves. I particularly like this book, as it includes a confidential online assessment of your EQ scores in these four areas, with guidance on how to improve your skills.

1.1 Self-awareness and personality assessments

Understanding yourself is the starting point for EQ. Self-awareness is important if we are to understand our reactions to other people.

Lawyers have a professional obligation to be aware of problems that may impair their ability, including psychological and emotional problems.

The HR teams in some law firms provide psychometric tests to help lawyers become aware of and understand their style compared to others – and to help them make the necessary adjustments to their behaviour so that they can work more effectively with others.

Some firms use personality tests such as the Myers-Briggs Type Inventory (MBTI).[53] The MBTI is based on Jungian psychology and classifies personalities into one of 16 types depending on the combination of four different spectra:

- introvert versus extrovert (I or E);
- sensory versus intuitive (S or N);
- thinking versus feeling (T or F); and
- judging versus perceiving (J or P).

Many lawyers fall into the ISTJ category.

Other firms use a Colour Insight[54] approach, which classifies people as red, blue, yellow or green. More recently, Deloitte developed a Business Chemistry[55] assessment which classifies people as pioneers, drivers, guardians or integrators.

Leadership and team development skills

Ben Evans is the founder of HumanTalk. He is a training and coaching specialist who has worked in management consultancy and not-for-profit organisations – including armed forces charity the Royal British Legion – on leadership and team development. He recently collaborated with Gill Steel, a leading private client solicitor and trainer, to host workshops with lawyers on managing challenging behaviour.

There can be a real tension around the discussion of 'soft skills'. They are some of the hardest skills to develop, because doing so requires recognising that results are so often determined by relationships. In most situations, no amount of technical expertise will make up for a lack of self-awareness, an inflexible communication style or an inability to convey genuine interest and concern for your client, colleague or team.

Fundamentally, developing soft skills is about humans learning to seek the best in each other regardless of how challenging the situation, and working with, rather than supressing or ignoring, our emotions. At its simplest level it is about human-to-human interaction.

With lawyers, are we expecting technical experts to understand how to manage people (let alone themselves) simply because of their length of service or mastery of the law? In my experience, lawyers are highly intelligent, competent professionals; but those who perhaps stand the best chance of excelling in the long term – particularly given changing client expectations and cultural norms

– are the lawyers who put in the effort to understand themselves and the fellow humans they lead, work for and support.

One useful approach, if handled properly by a qualified coach or trainer, can be using a psychometric such as Hogan®.[56] *By helping you gain insight into yourself – your values, motivations, behavioural preferences and even your dark side – psychometrics can help you lead a team or present to a client with greater levels of comfort and flexibility.*

Another angle to consider is the mental health and wellbeing of your team, your clients and – just as important – yourself. Working life and working relationships can be demanding, legal challenges and concerns stressful, and leadership a lonely existence. Leaders can benefit hugely from having a trusted adviser, coach or mentor who offers a safe space to process the ups and downs of leadership and provides support and challenge in equal measure. Given how contagious our emotions can be and how influential leaders are, healthy team performance often begins with healthy leadership.

The military makes a massive investment in training to develop leaders so that they can act professionally and effectively when deployed in demanding and unfamiliar environments. Technical expertise works hand in hand with the 'soft skills' of negotiation, effective communication and stress management.

Before you or your team is deployed on the next mission, it might serve you well to consider what levels of EQ, relational capability or personal resilience are required – not only for the benefit of your client (and ultimately your profits), but also for the health, wellbeing and contentment of you and your colleagues.

1.2 Self-management

Some people have a mental model of what constitutes 'professional' behaviour that excludes emotion, and thus suppress both positive and negative emotions as they work. But most people would agree that we need authentic people who are in touch with their emotions and can express them effectively. This is a vital ingredient of leadership.

Those with little ability to regulate their emotions can be unpredictable and even threatening to others. They have no filter – what they feel is what they express. Those who can self-manage are aware of what they are feeling and how it makes them act. They take a moment to understand what has triggered them, how to self-soothe and how to articulate themselves in a calm way. Those who maintain a consistent style and behaviour will earn the trust of those around them.

"Those who can self-manage are aware of what they are feeling and how it makes them act. They take a moment to understand what has triggered them, how to self-soothe and how to articulate themselves in a calm way. Those who maintain a consistent style and behaviour will earn the trust of those around them."

I have met lawyers who are really high in EQ, with a high degree of self-awareness and good self-management abilities under normal circumstances; but who lose some control when under pressure, becoming erratic and unpredictable.

1.3 Social awareness and empathy

Empathy – the ability to imagine things from other people's point of view and see things from other people's perspectives – is a critical skill for lawyers. Lawyers need to be able to tune into how colleagues, team members and clients might be feeling. Empathy is vital for all manner of activities, from communicating to building relationships and negotiating.

Psychologists Daniel Goleman and Paul Ekman[57] break down empathy into three categories:

- cognitive (you are aware of the feelings of others and what they might be thinking, but do not feel them directly);
- emotional (also known as affective empathy – you are able to share the feelings of another person); and
- empathic concern (also known as compassionate empathy – you are able to sense what another person needs from you and you take action accordingly).

Physician Shawn Shea argues that patients "are searching for someone who is trying to understand how they feel".[58] This is no different for many legal clients.

The importance of empathy
Geoffrey Lander is a non-executive chairman of Davitt Jones Bould. He was previously a property finance solicitor and head of the property department at Nabarro Nathanson (now part of CMS). At his peak, he was working 4,200 hours a year and generating £12.3 million.

> *Every call, email and document is an opportunity to impress, but it is also an opportunity to lose a client if:*
>
> - *calls are not returned in a timely manner;*
> - *calls are made at the wrong time of day;*
> - *emails include jargon or horrible acronyms (eg, 'BTW'); or*
> - *documents contain typos or the incorrect name of the client vehicle.*
>
> *You may call these soft skills; I call them common sense. I was a practising lawyer for 30 years and you know what I learned in my first six months out of private practice? Common sense is the least common of all senses! The biggest tip I can ever give anyone is, "Put yourself in the other person's shoes and decide what you would expect to hear or read if it were you."*

1.4 Relationship management

Once you have empathy, you need the ability to adjust your behaviour appropriately. EQ has a measurable psychological construct for how well you manage relationships. Obviously, this ability is important for lawyers – whether for internal or external relationships. The ability to assess which lawyers excel in this area makes it easier to choose them for leadership, business development and client relationship management roles.

An indicator of the growing importance of the topic is the recent launch by the *Harvard Business Review* of a series of short books on EQ.[59] Topics include authentic leadership, dealing with difficult people, empathy, happiness, influence and persuasion, leadership presence, mindfulness, purpose, meaning and passion and resilience.

1.5 Being politically astute

Most organisations – including law firms – have some form of internal politics. A key element of effective client management is navigating the internal political environment of client organisations.

In 2015 Jean Hartley, professor of public leadership at the Open Business School, considered people's ability to deal with politics in organisations.[60] She addressed this by looking at five distinct areas – many of which are reliant on highly developed EQ:

- personal skills – being self-aware, having self-control and curiosity about other people, and being proactive;
- interpersonal skills – making others feel valued, building relationships with a variety of people, encouraging people to talk to you, and having soft skills and tough skills such as negotiating and dealing with conflict;
- reading people and situations – getting people together to address the issues below the surface, understanding the power that people have, recognising when you might be perceived as a threat and using both analytical and intuitive skills;
- building alignment and alliances – reaching out to people to build collaboration, deciding who to include and exclude, going beyond the immediate and obvious partners and working across competing interests; and
- strategic direction and scanning – understanding your purpose and what you want to achieve, anticipating and timing things correctly.

"Put yourself in the other person's shoes and decide what you would expect to hear or read if it were you."

2. Client views on emotional intelligence in lawyers

Over the years, I have listened to many law firm clients at conferences and captured their comments relating to EQ in lawyers. Despite the passage of many years, the comments remain remarkably consistent and confirm that lawyers need to improve their EQ.

In 2010 the chairman of Better Capital said:

- "Body language, words and attention are important."
- "People playing with their BlackBerry is a turn-off. I need people to show that they are interested – with eye contact."

Also in 2010, the vice president of corporate real estate for Europe, the Middle East and Africa at JP Morgan said:

- "The relationship and chemistry are important – you need to know that the teams will work well together. The problem is when those who present are not those who are actually going to do the work."

In 2011 the associate general counsel Europe for Styron said:

- "There's no value in brands – I'm not looking at their website or brand. For commercial work, it's about relationships."
- "I instruct who I know personally – who I have met at a conference or pitch."

Also in 2011 the head of legal, United Kingdom, Ireland and South Africa, infomagnetic technologies counsel of IBM United Kingdom said:

- "Outside counsel must really get to know how we operate and there must be a good relationship and fit."
- "Treat your client as you would a friend – open communication and mutual benefit."

In 2012 the general counsel at the *Financial Times* said:

- "It is often about face time – delivering advice the old-fashioned way. Ask your partners, 'When was the last time you rang the client for no reason?'"
- "I always look at the staff – do they appear happy, motivated and enjoyable to work with? It's easier to deal with someone who is happy."

Also in 2012, the group general counsel of Nationwide Building Society said:

- "Face time is important, so that advisers can 'get' the client from

a cultural perspective – to understand our values and how we like to operate."
- "We spend a day sharing our strategy for the next year with our panel advisers. It takes commitment from both sides. But how many firms have sent partners to spend a few days walking around at client premises on the shop floor with our guys?"

In 2015 the in-house counsel at Argus Media said:

- "We're not made to feel special."
- "Some advisers have learned how to communicate with each individual person – being good at gauging different personalities. Some firms just deliver their advice without deploying their human skills to be aware of different personality types."

Also in 2015, a senior lawyer at Santander said:

- "Being a 'trusted adviser' means being pragmatic, engaging and proactive; knowing the regulatory framework and risks to our business; and thinking outside the box."
- "There is a partner in a City firm who is technically gifted, a great strategist and a good salesman. It's not just about the technical advice and not everyone has all the required skills."

In 2016 the CEO and founder of workplace design company FourFront Group said:

- "Rapport is important. I am amazed that the basics on pitches from lawyers and accountants are ignored – I have come to expect a flat, dull presentation with a bit of PowerPoint."
- "You have to know who you are presenting to – the individuals."
- "It's a given that all those pitching will meet the criteria; so you need to answer the question, 'Can I work with these people? Do I like and trust them?'"

In 2017 the CEO of the Chartered Institute of Marketing said:

- "Use the pitch to interrogate the client and their needs. It's not a selling session; it's a relationship session. A firm of solicitors recently pitched to a pension fund trustee, but hadn't rehearsed. You have to show both pride and passion in a pitch."
- "Understand the specific needs of the client and explain why you are in the room."

In 2018 the general counsel for the Crown Estate said:

- "Align with our aims by listening at the first meeting and

returning at a second meeting having absorbed and addressed our purpose and values."
- "Fundamentally it's about human interaction – people want to trust someone."
- "Invest in a long-term relationship – you may be talking to us for some time before you receive an instruction"

In 2018 the general counsel for JUUL Lab said:

- "EQ is important."
- "What stands out is kindness – firms that treat their staff well."
- "Ideally, I want a professional relationship with people I like and who, in time, become friends."

3. The link between confidence and perfectionism
Lawyers need to be confident. There is a difference between feeling self-confident (internal) and conveying confidence (external).

Self-confidence is connected to self-esteem. Self-esteem is something we develop when we are young – it's the difference between how we see ourselves (our self-image) and our 'perfect self', or how we think we should be. If parents criticise a child rather than his or her

"Many of those interviewed touched on the importance of mental wellbeing and resilience. This has become more acute as a result of isolation in lockdown during the coronavirus pandemic. Lawyers need the ability to minimise, recognise and address the symptoms of stress."

behaviour, the child will have low self-esteem. Labelling affects the person who is labelled – he or she begins to believe that label.

There are two models of self-esteem – the enclosed circle model and the linear model. Under the enclosed circle model, the individual is understood to be the most important person in his or her own life, and accepts that others are the most important people in their own. Enclosed circle people are reassured about the things that they are and do, and are not influenced by what other people do or think.

Under the linear model of self-esteem, an individual can feel good only by comparing himself or herself favourably with others. It involves a hierarchal mind-set, where everyone can't be equally good – instead, someone must be the best.

Perfectionists are people who have to get everything right – they have excessively high standards. Perfectionists have difficulty letting things go and varying their standards to the time available and the effort needed. Perfectionists often appear to be control freaks. Perfectionists often have unrecognised fears and needs – they are motivated by a fear of failure and are never satisfied by their achievements.

Perfectionists also keep their emotions hidden and fear showing vulnerability or losing control. Healthy people are motivated by enthusiasm and generally feel okay about themselves, show vulnerability and are not afraid to make mistakes.

Psychologist Brené Brown[61] observed that "Connection gives purpose and meaning to our lives", and pointed out that we are neuro-biologically wired to connect with people. We feel a sense of shame and fear at the prospect of disconnection, as it makes us feel unworthy. She also suggested that "what makes you vulnerable makes you beautiful", and advised that to support connection we should let ourselves be seen more clearly, which includes revealing some of our vulnerabilities. This relates to authenticity.

4. Stress, resilience and wellbeing

Many of those interviewed touched on the importance of mental wellbeing and resilience. This has become more acute as a result of isolation in lockdown during the coronavirus pandemic. Lawyers need the ability to minimise, recognise and address the symptoms of stress.

Resilience is the capacity to bounce back from setbacks and become a more capable and adaptive person. There are three aspects to resilience:[62]

- the ability to absorb stress and to continue functioning despite adversity;
- the ability to recover from untoward events; and
- the ability to learn and grow from previous episodes of resilient action.

Resilient people find meaning, value and impact in their work; think differently under stressful conditions; connect with others when stressed; and tend to be givers rather than takers.

The legal sector is a high-pressure environment – and never more so since the coronavirus pandemic. There are many initiatives aimed at helping lawyers to recognise and reduce the harmful impact of stress – the triggering of the 'fight, flight or freeze' response that floods the body with chemicals such as adrenaline and cortisol, which affects the immune and cardiovascular systems as well as mental health, if it occurs frequently. Such initiatives include mindfulness and meditation training, as well as resilience building and work-life balance awareness. Many firms have trained mental health first aiders or provide employee assistance programmes and confidential counselling services.

Stress is not necessarily about the amount of work or pressure we are dealing with, but rather how we react to it. Our response is affected to a degree by our personality. For example, some people might be emotional inhibitors (who bottle things up), emotional ruminators (who dwell on past upsets) or toxic achievers (with inappropriate competitiveness, time pressure, anger and hostility).

In their 'healthy mind platter',[63] David Rock and Dan Siegal offer seven essential daily mental activities for optimum brain health:

- focus time (addressing tasks and challenges in a goal-oriented way);
- play time (being spontaneous and creative; making new connections in the brain);
- connecting time (connecting with other people or the natural world);
- physical time (moving your body – the Center for Creative Leadership found a strong correlation between regular exercise and performance);[64]
- time in (quietly reflecting – focusing on sensations, images, feelings and thoughts);
- down time (letting your mind wander and relax, without goals); and
- sleep time.

A 2002 Harvard Business School report entitled *How Resilience Works*[65] suggested that there are three fundamental characteristics that set resilient people and organisations apart:

- the capacity to face reality;
- the ability to find meaning in testing times; and
- the ability to improvise.

General advice to increase your resilience includes the following:

- Maintain good relationships with family and friends.
- Avoid seeing crises or stressful situations as unbearable events.
- Accept circumstances that cannot be changed.
- Develop realistic goals and move towards them.
- Take decisions or actions in adverse situations.
- Look for opportunities for self-discovery after a struggle with loss.
- Develop self-confidence.
- Keep a long-term perspective and consider stressful events in a broader context.
- Maintain a hopeful outlook – expect good things.
- Take care of your mind and body – eat properly, exercise regularly and pay attention to your own needs and feelings.

Managing people

Janice Barber, a solicitor specialising in clinical negligence, was managing partner of leading health and social care firm Hempsons for many years. Hempsons has lawyers in offices at London, Manchester and Harrogate. She is now a non-executive director of the West London Mental Health Trust and two other health organisations.

There is a tidal wave of burnout heading towards the profession. This is caused by several things happening in parallel – the pressure to keep up with the constant change in the regulatory environment; increasingly sophisticated and demanding clients; the expectation that highly paid solicitors entering the profession will deliver strong financial results from the outset; and claims against lawyers skyrocketing.

The old culture of law firms had the belief that if you were seen to suffer from stress, you were someone who would need to be treated delicately and might not be considered for employment or promotion. You were expected to swim in shark-infested waters and show no signs of weakness.

Law firm leaders need to learn how best to manage high-

performance teams. We need training so that leaders are alert to and recognise the early signs of stress. They need to know how and when to intervene and provide assistance before it becomes a serious medical issue. Otherwise, by the time the affected lawyers approach HR or organisational development professionals, it is too late. We've always trained lawyers in health and safety and this must be extended to mental health protection of both legal and support staff.

I am passionate about this issue, both personally and professionally. In my early career, the work ethic was insane and I demanded extremely high standards from trainees. Of course, many of the people who I trained went on to have brilliant legal careers. But I constantly reflect on those who found the pace too much and disappeared. A different attitude to mental health may have retained those excellent people in the profession.

5. Decision making

Surprisingly, emotions play a key role in decision making. Even the most apparently rational decisions owe much to our emotions. Neuroscientists have found that people who have damage to the part of the brain concerned with emotions are unable to make decisions.

"We need a certain degree of stress to perform: too little and people become complacent; but too much and the pre-frontal cortex closes down, so we forget things and panic. Sufficient sleep is essential for consolidation of memory and aids our ability to make connections and improve decision making for insight-type problems."

Cognitive biases – of which there are hundreds – can also subconsciously affect decision making. There is significant new material on this topic and on 'nudging'.[66] Increased self-awareness and an understanding of how your brain reacts subconsciously can help ensure better decision making.

Decision fatigue describes a certain point in the day at which the quality of our decisions diminishes. A *New York Times* article[67] cites psychologist Roy Baumeister, who demonstrated that we have a finite store of mental energy for exerting self-control and making quality decisions.

David J Cresswell has shown that we make better decisions, especially when dealing with complex information, when a period of distraction is introduced.[68] Other psychologists have found that better group decisions are made when there is a diverse mix of people contributing.

6. High-performance environment

Dr Jessica Payne of the Neuroleadership Institute is a researcher on the role of sleep and stress on memory.[69] She has argued that we need a certain degree of stress to perform: too little and people become complacent; but too much and the pre-frontal cortex closes down, so we forget things and panic. Sufficient sleep is essential for consolidation of memory and aids our ability to make connections and improve decision making for insight-type problems.

A positive mood assists learning, memory, insight and executive brain functions, and enables understanding of a broader perspective. It becomes easier to make connections and solve problems more creatively.

V. Methods of developing lawyer soft skills

A recent *Harvard Business Review* article[70] reported:

> *Organisations spent $359 billion globally on training in 2016 but was it worth it? Not when you consider the following:*
>
> - *75% of 1,500 managers surveyed from 50 organisations were dissatisfied with their company's L&D function*
> - *70% of employees report that they don't have mastery of the skills needed to do their jobs*
> - *Only 12% of employees apply new skills learned in L&D programs to their jobs*
> - *Only 25% of respondents to a recent McKinsey survey believe that training measurably improved performance.*

The authors argued that people learn best when they have to learn. Neuroplasticity – also known as brain or neural plasticity – is the ability of the brain to change continuously throughout an individual's life.

Despite some cynicism about the effectiveness of training, law firms invest a significant amount in developing their lawyers, both during their two-year training contracts and throughout their careers. However, this may not be as much as is spent in some service businesses: for example, to sustain customer service excellence,

Singapore Airlines adopts the 40/30/30 rule[71] – 40% spent on training, 30% on improving procedures and 30% on creating new products.

1. Approaches to training and development

There are many different approaches to developing lawyer soft skills. Here we explore some of the most common methods.

1.1 Dedicated learning and development function

In larger law firms there is often an L&D function within the HR team. Sometimes, these functions are further split into legal (for apprentices and trainees, as well for more experienced lawyers), technology, business and soft skills.

In the largest firms, these function as sophisticated in-house learning consultancies – helping their boards to identify strategic skill gaps in their current and future workforce. They then apply a host of psychology-based tools to understand those gaps and find ways to provide the necessary training to help their firms succeed.

In smaller firms, the L&D professionals add rigour and process to skills training programmes and direct teams to the appropriate external resources to deliver that training.

But sadly, in many firms either there is either no L&D function at all or it operates in an administrative space – keeping records of training requirements, organising attendance at training events and managing processes such as annual skills appraisals.

In-house team uses learning and organisational development to drive integration and performance

Carolann Edwards is global director of learning and organisational development at Norton Rose Fulbright LLP.

Our global L&D team operates as an in-house consultancy. We conduct needs analysis, research content and design and deliver courses. We also undertake team studies, and build and run assessment centres. Psychometrics such as Hogan and MBTI form a key part of our development toolkit in our work with partners, associates and business services staff at all levels of seniority.

The global team includes a dozen team members who regularly deliver training. Our reputation for training is stellar and senior managers across the firm play an active part in developing our people by delivering sessions on the programmes we run, to ensure that everyone in the firm has the knowledge and skills they need to exceed our clients' expectations.

The team has won awards for its L&D strategy, leadership courses, coaching and cross-border work from a range of bodies, such as the Law Society England and Wales, the Managing Partners' Forum and the Training Journal.

The core curriculum

Since 2009, the firm has grown significantly as a result of seven combinations. The L&D team has played a pivotal role in helping the firm to integrate via a range of L&D projects and courses. For us, L&D is a strategic imperative and an organisational development tool which facilitates the transmission of culture and drives performance. It also helps us to achieve brand consistency and provide the same level of excellence in service delivery globally.

International academies are ensemble programmes and assessment and development centres, which cover a range of topics – including management and leadership – and last for between one and three days. There are six which align with a lawyer's career progression. Thus, newly qualified lawyers attend International Academy 1; and senior associates, counsel and special counsel attend International Academy 6. Each academy is geared to the work lawyers are doing day to day and provides information on the firm's structure, systems, processes and culture. Attendance at the international academies is compulsory for associates.

Our L&D curriculum for partners includes the annual new partners' conference for internally promoted partners and lateral hires. One of its key objectives is to foster collaboration. The International Academy for Partners includes programmes for those at the start of their career as partners, as well as those who are more senior and responsible for leading teams.

Masterclasses are short courses of up to three hours which address a single topic such as work management, creativity, negotiation skills, presentations and project management. They provide focused knowledge and skills to partners and associates who want to learn more about a particular topic.

The in-house lawyer curriculum

As a firm providing legal services, our core strengths are in financial institutions; energy; transport; infrastructure; mining and commodities; life sciences and healthcare; and technology and innovation. It is perhaps no surprise that many of our clients operate in those sectors. We are proud to train their lawyers too.

Clients participate in our masterclasses and they value them highly. The feedback on the training we get from clients is great. They like what we do because the courses are lawyer and business centric.

Our "In Law" series of courses has been specifically designed by our L&D team to meet the needs of in-house legal teams. There are three programmes that follow the progression of in-house lawyers.

"Leaders in Law" is for general counsel of a region or business unit who are comparatively new to the role. "Future Leaders in Law" is a talent programme aimed at developing the next generation of general counsel. "Managers in Law" is for in-house lawyers who have recently joined from private practice and those who are at the earliest stage of managing others. The "In Law" series is a global offering. Courses have run in Frankfurt, Hong Kong, Houston, Johannesburg, London, Paris, Singapore and Sydney, where they have been really well received. Clients hugely appreciate these programmes because they feel that we 'get' in-house lawyers.

The L&D team also tailors courses for clients by leveraging the knowledge of training design and pedagogy that some team members have acquired via specialist professional qualifications in L&D. Our training is experiential and activity based, drawing on real situations.

Diversity

In 2009 we designed the Careers Strategies Programme for high-potential female associates. This year is the tenth anniversary of the programme's launch. Its aim was to increase the number of female partners in London from 13%. It is now 27% – a great achievement. However, we are not complacent and are working hard to increase that number further. The programme is now run globally in North America, London and Australia, with delegates travelling to the nearest region to participate. Topics covered include leadership, self-knowledge and evaluation, political savvy, sponsorship and partner promotions – the steps.

Our Black, Asian and Minority Ethnic Careers Strategies Programme launched successfully in London in 2019. The topics covered on the programme include leadership derailers, difficult conversations, stakeholder management, career focus and planning and personal brand. This programme is also for high potentials and we have great hopes for it.

Online learning

Online learning is one area in which we have not made a big splash. Given our taste for innovation, this is somewhat surprising. However, I feel that the demand for it is not as high as futurists and other commentators had anticipated. As a result, we provide the basics, such as e-learning courses covering risk and compliance issues; but not a lot else. To some extent, we have also been put off by the dearth of technology that lends itself to the type of activity-based, skills development training we provide face to face, which our people value. When the technology improves, we'll do more electronic learning, provided that our internal and external clients demand it and use it in numbers that warrant the opportunity and financial costs.

More than once I have been told that our L&D function is one of the 'jewels in the crown' of the firm. To the extent that people feel that this is so is a credit to the firm for its long investment in L&D, the team itself and the active interest and involvement of colleagues and clients at all levels of seniority.

"Some firms have sophisticated and integrated training academies which demonstrate what competencies are required at each level of seniority, and have courses, modules and information to aid the selection of the appropriate training."

1.2 Training academies

Some firms have sophisticated and integrated training academies which demonstrate what competencies (see p 69) are required at each level of seniority, and have courses, modules and information to aid the selection of the appropriate training.

Larger firms will also have professionals who conduct regular training needs analysis and ensure that the training offering supports the needs identified through the ongoing staff appraisal process. These people will often look at other professions and sectors to see what can be learned from best practice. They will talk to clients and scan the horizon to see what future skills might be needed and provide early interventions to ensure their development. They will see the changing skills requirements as an opportunity to differentiate rather than a threat to be reduced.

One large firm publishes a skills academy schedule – underpinned by a competency framework – with courses in areas such as people and performance management, financial/commercial, technical ability, know-how and training, compliance and risk, client relationship management and business development. Within the people category, there are courses on email writing, time management, feedback, supervision, delegation, coaching and mentoring, performance management and building and leading great teams. Within the client services and business development category, skills courses include adopting a sector approach, cross-selling, client interviewing, challenging conversations, bringing in business, networking, acting as a trusted adviser, personal impact, presenting with impact, media presence and chairing.

1.3 External training suppliers

Smaller firms will purchase the majority of their training from external suppliers – there are several commercial organisations (see p 178) that specialise in providing public and in-house courses for lawyers.

An increasing number of conferences and seminars are organised by legal associations, networks of lawyers, the media (eg, *The Lawyer* and *Legal Business*) and other commercial ventures that provide training and development opportunities.

However, not all external training providers are aware of the particular culture and needs of lawyers. They need to speak the language of the lawyers they are training and have real empathy with the demands and constraints they face on a daily basis. External providers may also struggle to integrate their training with the other development activities of the firm.

"Not all external training providers are aware of the particular culture and needs of lawyers. They need to speak the language of the lawyers they are training and have real empathy with the demands and constraints they face on a daily basis."

LawNet: training, learning and development programmes for lawyers[72]

LawNet has 70 member firms ranging in size from £2m – £25m. A major benefit for members is access to an extensive training programme with over 50 face-to-face learning events covering a range of topics:

- Legal updates
- Skills development
- Leadership, management and strategy
- Marketing & business development
- Compliance & risk management
- Business support

Within skills development there is negotiation, writing and drafting, advocacy and coaching. Marketing topics have included the effective use of social media, demonstrating value to a client and preparing bid documents.

1.4 Self-managed learning

Much of the development of hard and soft skills relies on lawyers learning on their own initiative. This requires a great deal of motivation. While this is an effective way to absorb knowledge –

through books and other written and video materials – acquiring the relevant skills often involves activities, role play, practice and working alongside others.

However, the importance of self-development and learning can get lost in the pressures of urgent client demands and fee-earning targets. And it is a big ask to expect lawyers to know how to assess what soft skills they need and how best to develop them. They require expert advice, systems and processes and constant reminders to maintain an open approach to continuous development.

A skills framework for associates, coaching and feedback
Jamie Butler was a solicitor at Clifford Chance before moving into training and L&D at BPP Law School, Russell-Cooke and CMS. Most recently he was director of L&D at Cleary Gottlieb Steen & Hamilton LLP. He is also a certified coach.

There had always been an appetite and motivation for technical skills training here, but soft skills training had been rather piecemeal and ad hoc. I started with a learning needs analysis for both associates and business support staff. The first part of this was an easy-to-use, structured online questionnaire asking for importance ratings on a suite of soft skills.

Then we arranged focus groups for newly qualified lawyers, those with three to five years' experience and those with more than five years' experience. There were some surprises – for example, the high interest in project management skills among junior lawyers. Perhaps that reflects on the early responsibility we give to our lawyers.

Preferred delivery methods
We also explored the preferred method of training delivery. There was a desire to provide regular short bursts of intense training – keeping face-to-face workshop time to a minimum (60 to 90 minutes) with no more than 12 delegates to encourage interaction.

This means that we assign advance reading, research and/or scenario preparation before sessions, with blended learning (eg, videos, alternative models, online resources) and reflection afterwards. This allows the workshops to be experiential and highly interactive. and provides plenty of opportunity to practise skills in dyads and triads. No more 'chalk and talk' sessions or 'death by PowerPoint'!

Tiered and modular soft skills programme
We designed a tiered and modular training programme. The initial

offering had 12 modules, including negotiation, project management, influencing and persuasion, business development, networking, coaching and feedback. After the first year of roll-out, we revised the LPM training into three modules: increasing knowledge, skills and opportunities for application. The structure remains flexible so that we can add further detail and depth to topics as required.

I deliver around 50% of the training myself, alongside a small group of external facilitators and coaches. And we have partnered with people from whom we license high-quality video resources onto our intranet.

Supporting training with coaching sessions

We also support legal and business support staff with coaching programmes. Some are executive coaching programmes with up to six sessions and others are shorter programmes with perhaps only three.

We also arrange 'coaching conversation' days, where anyone in the office can book an hour's slot – these are particularly popular after mid-year and end-of-year reviews. But we have also seen a lot of people come to those coaching sessions following the workshops as they practise applying the techniques to their own situations or consolidate their learning.

Future skills development

The firm recently appointed a global chief talent officer in New York and I'm sure this will bring a more holistic approach to our L&D programmes internationally – redressing the balance between legal and other skills.

We are seeing some of our soft skills development work being transferred back into our client work – for example, applying them when delivering training courses for our clients. That's particularly valuable with the whole human skills palette.

We have also started upskilling everyone in key areas. For example, we've spent a lot of time building feedback skills among the legal and business support teams. This we hope will encourage a more regular day-to-day feedback culture and develop broader coaching skills among our managers and leaders.

Ultimately, I hope we move to a more self-directed learning model, where legal and support staff will select what they need to learn from a rich variety of traditional and digital learning resources.

1.5 Best practice

Many firms will have detailed documentation provided by experts and the most experienced practitioners – incorporated into practice management and case management systems – that incorporates the relevant knowledge and skills for lawyers to acquire.

While these are usually focused on technical skills, the advent of technology such as AI and machine learning increasingly means that soft skills can also be learned this way. A good example is the on-boarding process, where the user is prompted to consider the quality of the client experience and interaction cues are provided.

Some firms have invested in systems (eg, Intapp) that intelligently assess the available data – sometimes pulled automatically from email exchanges and meeting notes – to prompt lawyers to make client relationship interventions and will even provide suggested scripts for them to use.

1.6 On-the-job training

There are two approaches here. The passive model expects younger lawyers to absorb the required skills simply by working among more experienced lawyers – almost by osmosis. This assumes both that those younger lawyers will have the necessary observational and analytical skills (as well as the motivation), and that the role models they are following are exhibiting the appropriate behaviours.

The more active approach involves being supervised, trained and coached by more senior lawyers. It assumes that the senior lawyers have sufficient skills in these areas and have the motivation and time to devote to developing younger lawyers. It also presupposes that the senior lawyers are proficient at transferring these skills to others. Training, motivation, delegation, coaching and feedback skills are therefore core requirements for those lawyers responsible for the development of others.

This is one area of training that has been particularly hard hit by the requirement to work from home during the coronavirus crisis. The lack of physical proximity means that the frequent, casual conversations among teams of lawyers that can be so valuable for sharing ideas and skills no longer take place. New skills in how to facilitate this informal team collaboration digitally have become increasingly important as a result.

1.7 Case studies and scenario analysis

Back in 1964, Dale Carnegie said: "Learning is an active process. We learn by doing."[73] The Harvard Business School pioneered the use of the case method – a case study-based method of learning. The advantage of case studies is that knowledge and skills are applied to a real-life scenario.

Case studies and role play are common methods of supporting lawyer training. They are also effective methods of building collaboration and team-working skills. Moot or mock courts are frequently used to develop legal and advocacy skills, and are also a good forum for developing more nuanced soft skills.

New technology – involving online collaboration, apps and real-time simulations and notifications, and providing alternative outcomes depending on chosen strategies and actions – is likely to make this method of training more popular.

1.8 Peer learning

Researchers have found that when employees want to learn new skills, 55% of them ask a colleague for help.

Humans tend to learn as they teach, so peer learning offers a way to support rapid, just-in-time learning. Firms can implement a range of measures to encourage and facilitate peer-to-peer learning, such as online collaboration, workshops, active learning groups and buddy systems.

However, the effectiveness of these measures presupposes some cultural requirements: people being trained in how to train and recognition for time invested in training others.

1.9 Secondments and shadowing

Trainee solicitors spend time in different practice groups as part of their training. Yet although they have both training and relationship benefits, internal and external secondments are rarer for those later in their legal careers. Some firms are nervous about secondments to client organisations – due to both cost implications and the fear that secondees might 'go native' and join the secondment organisation on a permanent basis.

Yet joining another team – even for a short period, such as a week – can provide an immersive, concentrated and effective training experience if it is structured and managed well. Shadowing – where a lawyer works alongside another person – can also take place over a much shorter period.

1.10 Part-time (voluntary) roles

As part of a leadership development programme, some firms encourage senior associates and junior partners to take part-time voluntary roles (eg, governor, trustee or non-executive director) in the third sector. These roles give lawyers direct experience of working with a board and insights into a range of management skills.

Lawyers who take these positions also gain in-depth knowledge of the sector, which can be invaluable in later market positioning and business development activities. Excellent training in sector-specific and management skills is usually provided as part of the arrangement.

However, the time investment and potential conflicts often deter firms from considering these opportunities.

1.11 Digital training and e-learning

The use of digital training resources continues to grow: some estimates forecast that the global e-learning market will be valued at $275 billion by 2022. Videos, podcasts, webinars and online tutorials are common and more easily accessible now that most people have smart phones that allow training to take place outside the office and on the move.

The coronavirus pandemic has put much travel on hold and halted physical gatherings of people, which rules out many traditional methods of training. As result, a significant investment is being made

"The coronavirus pandemic has put much travel on hold and halted physical gatherings of people, which rules out many traditional methods of training. As result, a significant investment is being made in developing sophisticated teleconferencing, telepresence, online collaboration and digital training resources."

in developing sophisticated teleconferencing, telepresence, online collaboration and digital training resources. It is likely that advances in this area will completely disrupt professional, technical and personal skills development. However, some argue that while digital methods of learning are effective for knowledge transfer training activities, they are less so for skills development.

The increase in digital training will require more than remote working and virtual team management skills. It will also demand a range of new soft skills, such as screen presence (performance skills), the ability to connect emotionally with people remotely and the ability to promote effective interaction.

TED talks are a popular way to acquire new knowledge – albeit not necessarily targeted at the legal sector. TED offers a vast array of topics covered in short videos (around 15 minutes) by leading subject-matter experts. The TED formula for presentations means that the videos are entertaining, engaging and educational.

OpenLearn[74] – a digital training resource from the Open University – provides a diverse range of high-quality learning resources, including lectures, videos, documents and interactive quizzes, as well as learning records. And it is entirely free. I have been impressed with topics on this programme on subjects as varied as coaching, digital literacy, facilitating, forensic psychology, managing relationships, mental health, leadership and working in diverse teams.

Training technology also allows for a high degree of interaction – for example, bots for instant messaging or chatting with training supervisors – and assessments to ensure that learning has taken place. I have been impressed by the high quality of soft skills CPD training resources offered by online CPD application QDooz; and there are many other similar systems on the market.

Psychology and technology in the delivery of soft skills training

Mark Day is the CEO and Sara Palmer is the L&D manager at Law South, a member-owned network of 12 mid-sized law firms with a combined income of £203 million, with 2,700 staff and more than 1,600 lawyers.

> *We have been providing training needs analysis and soft skills training to lawyers for more than 30 years – our content has really evolved over time. We assess and investigate the training needs, design the training requirement and then source the appropriate providers so that the members get training that is bespoke to their needs.*

Wide range of soft skills training topics

In the last six months we have provided more than 40 training courses both for all members and in-house for specific firms. Two-thirds of these were on soft skills.

The topics on which we provide soft skills training include assertiveness, communication, critical thinking, EQ, influencing, managing client relationships, mentoring, negotiation, networking, personal impact and winning new business. Recent training on social media marketing was also popular.

Some firms – despite doing a lot of supervision training – continue to notice failures in supervision, which raises questions about why behaviour didn't change enough. So we are speaking to educationalists and psychologists about how to modify the training delivery to really embed the right behaviours.

Many member firms have developed their own competency frameworks. We align with this and are looking to develop frameworks to structure our training provision for different levels of seniority and work focus. This will help firms avoid a piecemeal and ad hoc approach to training and consider the bigger picture of developing the right skills for the right type of future workforce.

Survey on coaching and change management

Our board members are managing a lot of change and we are helping them to see the links between strategy, organisational design and development, change management and training and coaching.

Identifying that coaching is one tool that can be used to help manage change, we recently surveyed members on their coaching activity. Our research showed the importance of coaching for issues as wide ranging as performance management and talent development.

We worked with leading coaching consultancy OCM Group, which analysed the results and was able to provide benchmarks and best practice information for the participants. We are following up with members to identify how else we may support them, such as sourcing qualified coaches for firms.

E-learning platforms

For many years, we have used e-learning to help with risk and compliance training. The size of our member firms means that they would be unlikely to have the resources to investigate and develop their own online learning content platforms, so we are looking at ways to help with this.

Options include working with an online training partner to make all of its content available to our members. It may be possible to use secure partitions for them to upload their own learning resources, although we do encourage them to share.

We recently worked with New Wave Learning, which uses an app to provide presentation skills training. It involved face-to-face sessions, specific times to dial in, coaching and prompts to review content, including TED talks. Lawyers could access the programme at any time of the day. It was so successful that we plan to run another cohort again soon.

We've also done some work with psychologists and leading law firm Schillings on cybersecurity around phishing emails. We are currently evaluating two providers of subscription services to online resources, learning modules and simulations to help firms refresh, reinforce and embed cyber-risk behaviours. These systems use cybertech experts and psychologists and deploy AI and machine learning to recognise the learning styles of users and adapt the system automatically for maximum learning effectiveness.

Current topics of interest

A recent topic of interest was "Having difficult conversations", encompassing discussions with both colleagues and clients, face to face and on the telephone. Obviously, empathy and EQ play a large part in training on managing challenging conversations.

Wellbeing and resilience are also hot topics. We provide resilience training as part of our Professional Skills Course for trainee solicitors. This addresses the difference between pressure and stress. Our members have done their own in-house training, often in conjunction with mental health charity Mind, with programmes for mental health first aid training and dementia friends training.

Looking forward, we see increased demand for training around process improvement (eg, Six Sigma and Lean), incorporating the client voice in process changes, systems analysis, analysing business needs and innovation. Some of the techniques, such as "Five Whys" questioning, are also relevant to group work on risk reduction. At two of our firms, the former managing partners have evolved into innovation and strategic change roles.

1.12 Role models

Regardless of what training is provided, it is natural that young lawyers will emulate those to whom they report and those who are more senior and seen as most successful in the practice.

Training can be ineffective if young lawyers return to their day jobs to find that senior people adopt a different approach. This suggests that training programmes must include the most senior members of the firm, who are sometimes among the hardest group to reach and engage on training programmes.

1.13 Feedback

The best leaders provide constant feedback to those they are managing. They emphasise positive feedback to provide psychological safety and build confidence. The recent Project Aristotle at Google[75] showed that high-performance teams exhibited psychological safety, dependability, structure and clarity, meaning and impact.

Unfortunately, the legal culture often focuses on correcting wrong behaviours rather than celebrating successful behaviours. There is more focus on the stick than the carrot, which can make people feel insecure and under attack, so they stop learning or taking risks.

Feedback is essential in helping people to identify and correct unconscious behaviours – known sometimes as 'blindspots' in the Johari Windows model. Joseph Lufts and Harry Ingham created the Johari Windows model[76] to show the importance of the need for exposure and feedback, as illustrated in Table 2.

Table 2. The Johari Windows model

	Known to self	Unknown to self
Known to others	Arena	Blind spot
Unknown to others	Façade	Unknown

Most firms have appraisal systems where formal feedback is provided against targets, key performance indicators (KPIs) and job descriptions. Some firms will have processes where 360-degree feedback is obtained from juniors, peers and seniors, for a more rounded view.

Many firms have client listening programmes where feedback from clients is also used as a development tool. Some firms use a system called Performance Leader,[77] which allows clients to provide instant

"Some firms use a system called Performance Leader, which allows clients to provide instant feedback on the performance of both the firm and individuals. This information provides a constant stream of feedback to individuals rather than simply at agreed annual appraisal times."

feedback on the performance of both the firm and individuals. This information provides a constant stream of feedback to individuals rather than simply at agreed annual appraisal times.

The subject of feedback is discussed further on p 140.

1.14 Coaching and mentoring

Many people interviewed for this report mentioned the importance of coaching and mentoring.

Coaching usually follows a structured process of asking questions so that the individual learns to think for himself or herself. Some professional qualified coaches specialise in helping lawyers; and many law firms provide basic coaching skills training to their lawyers to support internal coaching schemes.

Mentoring typically involves a more experienced person sharing his or her knowledge, wisdom and advice. However, it can be challenging for these people to find the time to mentor.

A key advantage of coaching and mentoring is that the learning is generally one to one and the individual's particular needs and style can be accommodated. However, this may be an expensive option.

Training at Davitt Jones Bould

Peter Allinson has been CEO at Davitt Jones Bould (DJB) for 20 years, before which he was a leader in industry. The firm is the largest specialist real estate law firm in the United Kingdom, with 22 partners and 100 staff based in offices in London, Manchester, Birmingham and Taunton.

Having spent many years in industry, I was amazed that lawyers referred to 'soft skills' when these are some of the hardest core skills to acquire. Without soft skills, there can be no success. Everyone needs to know how to organise their day with time management and communicate well as an individual when facilitating meetings with colleagues and clients. And leaders must know how to delegate, develop new business and be commercial and strategic, or they can't grow the firm. These are not things that are taught at university.

At DJB, we organise skills into four categories:

- *technical;*
- *personal development;*
- *organisational; and*
- *compliance and regulatory.*

In industry, we used FPOC (Forecast. Plan. Organise. Control); and when a young lawyer has an issue, I still use this framework to identify where the problem has occurred and how to fix it in future. One of the areas that we focus skills development on is thinking, situation analysis and problem-solving skills. I'm a great fan of Edward de Bono's books in this area.[78]

Lawyers are very bright. They were often top of their class. But this academic excellence can lead to an innate arrogance that looks down on skills in areas such as management, marketing, technology or HR. Sometimes, though, lawyers have unconscious incompetence – they are unaware of the skills they lack. I had a former boss who insisted that you couldn't train people who hadn't had a go at the job for this reason – they needed to recognise the need for many soft skills.

The book Good to Great *by Jim Collins*[79] *is a great leadership development book; and on personal effectiveness, you can't beat Stephen Covey's* Seven Habits of Highly Effective People.[80] *When working in industry, I learned the saying, "Leaders are not to be served, but to serve." I am constantly reading books to keep up to date with the latest management ideas and skills – I have a duty to be the leader our people deserve.*

An important role for leaders is to identify the core values of a business and embed them firmly in the culture, and navigate change management programmes around them. But most important of all is to have a deep sense of care for the team and individuals in the organisation, to make any training in skills meaningful. If the heart isn't in the right place, training is like applying sticking plasters to mortal wounds. Furthermore, people will tell that you are managing them according to a formula, rather than leading them.

The firm's strong commitment to lawyer training led it to develop an innovative online learning portal – DJB Learning[81] – which curates written and video training resources supporting the development of technical and soft skills for lawyers and surveyors in real estate. The firm is now leveraging this training expertise and resource to add value for its contacts, clients and referrers.

2. Law Society research

In July 2019 the SRA released a report[82] showing how law firms and solicitors have responded to the continuing competence requirement. Table 3 shows the most common types of training that firms have provided since it was introduced.

Table 3. Types of training delivered by firms to fulfil the continuing competence requirement

Internal approaches	%	External approaches	%
Reading, research and discussion	75	Training course on specific topics or areas of law	70
Informal training/on-the-job training	69	E-learning and webinars	59
Peer-to-peer informal learning	51	Conferences and events	58
Mentoring and coaching	48	L&D networks	30
Shared learning	39	Study towards a professional qualification or certification	23
E-learning and bespoke courses	44	Social media learning platforms	19
Secondments to other departments	5		

Whatever method of L&D is adopted – and there is a strong case for blended methods – you need to understand the principles of learning theory and how different people learn most effectively and efficiently. Learning styles are explored in the next section.

3. How to promote learning and different learning styles

It is helpful to consider the key learning theories to see how soft skills development can be optimised. These ideas are also valuable for managing change programmes.

3.1 Fear of change

Schein[83] argued that we engage in learning activity only when learning anxiety (the fear of learning something new) is outweighed by survival anxiety (the pressure to change). He explained that there are four types of fear to overcome, which may be particularly relevant for older and more experienced lawyers:

- fear of temporary incompetence;
- fear of punishment for incompetence;
- fear of loss of personal identity; and
- fear of loss of group membership.

"People with a fixed mind-set assume that intelligence and talents are innate – that you are born with them. Growth mind-set people assume that they can improve through working hard, practice and learning, so they explore and persist."

3.2 Fixed and growth mind-set

Carol Dweck[84] argued that people have either a fixed mind-set or a growth mind-set. People with a fixed mind-set assume that intelligence and talents are innate – that you are born with them. Growth mind-set people assume that they can improve through working hard, practice and learning, so they explore and persist.

3.3 Adaptive third

Psychologist Salvatore Maddi[85] found that creativity, insight and originality are more likely to come from people who enjoy stimulating experiences and fluctuating environments. This is the "openness to experience" characteristic of the 'Big Five' personality assessments (see p 91). With fellow researcher Carl Horn, he found that through a period of intense change management in a commercial organisation, one-third of people ("the adaptive third") thrived, while the majority suffered.

The simple difference in behaviour of the adaptive third was that while everyone else looked back at what had happened and why, they were focused on the future. Maddi described this as "existential courage".

This links to work by Silver,[86] who studied victims of bereavement, abuse and terrorism. She found in studies over many decades that a consistent one in three trauma victims will not search for a reason to explain why he or she is experiencing misfortune.

3.4 Change management

There are many excellent books on change management and the role of training interventions. In all models there is a need for clear vision, leadership, communication, engagement and training.

One of my favourite models (from Chip and Dan Heath in *Switch: How to Change when Change is Hard*)[87] describes the three elements required for any behaviour change:

- the rational reason;
- the emotional motivation; and
- the first small, specific action that must be taken.

I would also recommend Campbell MacPherson's *The Change Catalyst*[88] for a modern and comprehensive approach to the topic. There's also some excellent insight for leaders in *Neuroscience for Organizational Change* by Hilary Scarlett.[89]

3.5 Learning theory and process

Neuroscience shows that we have two ways of reacting to the world and change:

- our reflexive system, which is automatic and based on habit; and
- our reflective system, which is thoughtful and mindful.

Kevin Ochsner,[90] among others, estimates that humans act on habit 70% to 90% of the time. To change, people need to create a new habit by:

- setting goals;
- creating a strategy; and
- maintaining the personal motivation to change.

Charles Jennings' 70:20:10 Learning Model[91] posits that:

- 70% of actual learning is through experience (actual practice; on-the-job training);
- 20% is through exposure to informal, social learning and coaching; and
- only 10% is through formal classroom courses and other education.

There is a popular model of competency[92] that shows the stages through which people progress as they learn:

- unconscious incompetence – unaware that you are unable to do something;
- conscious incompetence – aware that you are unable to do something;
- conscious competence – improved performance as you work hard at the new thing you have learned; and
- unconscious competence – high performance where you act in a natural, automatic way.

David Kolb[93] suggested that to learn, we must progress through a four-stage cycle:

- concrete experience – we actually experience something (feeling);
- reflective observation – we think about something that happened (watching);
- abstract conceptualisation – we think about a future situation or possibility (planning); and
- active experimentation – we have a go at trying to do something (doing).

During this learning process, we use different types of thinking:

- diverging – considering new ideas to what we know during concrete experience and reflective observation;

- assimilating – incorporating new knowledge into internal mental models during reflective observation and abstract conceptualisation;
- converging – bringing things together and drawing conclusions during abstract conceptualisation and active experimentation; and
- accommodating – expanding existing mental models to make room for new ideas during active experimentation and concrete experience.

This means that the popular 'chalk and talk' knowledge-sharing approach to training is of limited value. Those designing training programmes need to understand how people learn best and tailor training experiences to incorporate the different learning processes and styles.

3.6 Learning styles

A variant of this model is provided by Peter Honey,[94] who suggested that there are differences in how people prefer to learn:

- Activists like to get on and experience something;
- Reflectors like to review what has happened;

"In learning, general concepts are easier to remember than details – so when introducing a new idea, our brains grasp the big picture of what we are learning rather than the details."

- Theorists tend to form conclusions about what has happened; and
- Pragmatists prefer to plan what they might do.

So in an ideal learning situation, there will be a mix of activities that appeal to these different preferences. It is also good to strengthen your own ability in those methods that are not your preference.

In learning, general concepts are easier to remember than details – so when introducing a new idea, our brains grasp the big picture of what we are learning rather than the details.

Traditionally, we learn through 'block practice', where we focus on a single topic for a while. Researcher Bob Bjork[95] found that interleaving learning is better for information retention and recollection. This suggests that you might switch between topics when learning.

3.7 Reflection

All learners need time to reflect, to allow the new information to become embedded. The process for reflective thinking is as follows:

- Description – what happened?
- Feelings – what were you thinking and feeling?
- Evaluation – what was good and bad about the experience?
- Analysis – what sense can you make of the situation?
- Conclusion – what else could have been done?
- Action plan – if it arose again, what would you do?

This follows the dynamics of the reflective space, which moves between internal and external energy for disaggregation, framing, implication analysis, insight, reframing, options and action. It is interesting that many CPD programmes (eg, the Chartered Institute of Marketing) require professionals to produce detailed reflection statements as evidence of their learning.

3.8 Retention

Psychologist Hermann Ebbinghaus[96] developed the 'forgetting curve', which shows retention rates of 58% after 20 minutes, 28% after two days and just 21% after 31 days. He found that if new information is not applied, we will forget 75% of it after just six days.

Hebb's Law (1949)[97] suggests that the more we do something, the easier it gets. Repetition strengthens synaptic connections: "Cells that fire together wire together."

Our brains quickly forget what we don't use. Incorporating new learning into your work is one way to retain knowledge. Another is

"Studies show that by using spaced repetition, we can remember about 80% of what we learn after 60 days. Neuroscientist Matthieu Boisgontier says that this is because our brains quickly forget what we do not use, in order to conserve energy."

spaced repetition: this was originally proposed by psychologist Cecil Alec Mace[98] in 1932 and refers to spreading learning out over time (material should be reviewed in gradually increasing intervals of roughly one day, two days, four days and eight days).

This approach takes advantage of the psychological spacing effect, which demonstrates a strong link between periodic exposure to information and retention. Studies show that by using spaced repetition, we can remember about 80% of what we learn after 60 days. Neuroscientist Matthieu Boisgontier[99] says that this is because our brains quickly forget what we do not use, in order to conserve energy.

Another approach is lean learning, which involves the following steps:

- Learn the core of what you need to learn (Tim Ferriss, author of *The Four Hour book* series,[100] suggests identifying the minimum learnable unit and applying the Pareto Principle – focus on the 20% of content that is used 80% of the time);
- Apply it immediately to real-world situations;
- Receive immediate feedback and refine your understanding; and
- Repeat the cycle.

This approach is frequently seen in law firm training workshops, where participants are given real-world scenarios to examine and address as part of the learning process.

A combination of verbal and visual material has been shown to deliver 85% recollection after three hours and 65% after three days. This is possibly because the nerves from the eye to the brain are 25 times larger than those from the ear to the brain, so 85% of information is absorbed visually.

3.9 Motivation to learn

Motivation is a key subject in its own right. However, with regard to development, I found the book *Helping People Change: Coaching with Compassion for Lifelong Learning and Growth*[101] most useful. The authors offer simple key messages – notably the power of visualising your ideal self and future vision to generate a 'positive energy attractor' (PEA).

The authors suggest focusing on strengths rather than correcting weaknesses or ensuring compliance with externally sourced targets, which triggers a 'negative energy attractor' (NEA) – a stress response from considering what we ought or should do. They argue that the desire to change must outweigh the obligation to change.

Their 'intentional change theory' involves the following stages:

- Identify the ideal self and personal vision;
- Explore the real self – both strengths and weaknesses;
- Establish a learning agenda;
- Experiment with and practise new behaviour; and
- Maintain resonant relationships and social identity groups based on mindfulness, a positive emotional tone, the arousal of hope, authentic connection and compassion.

The authors state: "To make changes stick, our research shows that it has to be intentionally and internally motivated rather than imposed from the outside."

4. Competency frameworks

Various case studies in this report indicate how law firms have consolidated and integrated all their skills requirements into a structure or a competency framework. There are also illustrative models in Appendix I (p 179).

Using competency frameworks

Sue Colton, director and founder of SJC Consulting, is an organisational development consultant who was previously employed by KPMG and NatWest and now works with blue-chip financial and professional services companies and leading not-for-profits in psychometric and behaviour assessment for staff selection and development.

> *Soft skills are the key differentiator for humans from automation and AI – machines can be taught knowledge and technical skills. Soft skills are innate and form the basis of drive and motivation. Competencies help us define and articulate what cultural values look like as desired behaviours. While a job description states 'what' you need to know to do the job (ie, the technical expertise), the competencies describe 'how' the job ideally should be done. It is said that it takes 18 months to change behaviour into sustained, consistent actions.*
>
> *With competencies, everyone knows what good looks like, through creating a clear line of sight as to the required outcomes.*
>
> *There are many benefits of using competency frameworks:*
>
> - *They link the individual's role more clearly to that of the business overall, increasing personal ownership of goals and objectives.*
> - *They play a major part in attracting and retaining staff, and underpin many people management principles such as recruitment, selection, recognition and development approaches.*
> - *They create a transparent and consistent way of measuring individual performance across the practice, providing more in-depth/focused performance and development discussions to take place on an ongoing basis.*
> - *Behavioural skills are transferable across all roles and professions, and can aid individual and business level career development planning.*
>
> *There are several ways to design a competency framework, depending on the complexity required and the size of the practice. An example of a detailed framework appears in the first table in Appendix I (see p 179), comprising a set of nine core competency headings that could be used across the business, together with a further four competencies specific to the senior management team that focus more on business growth and other widely recognised leadership qualities.*

The competency is then broken down into levels, incorporating explicit and progressive behavioural statements; an example of one competency appears in Appendix I.

Each similar role will have around seven competencies assigned to it, and then the relevant competency level attached will depend on the seniority of the role. Using the first person (ie, "I have..", "I give..") makes it more transparent when assessing people's abilities. It also creates opportunities to seek input from others, as the statements are clear and action orientated, and can equally be used within a 360-degree development tool if required.

From my observations having worked with lawyers, this group excels at analytical thinking and evidence-based decision making. Equally, critical reasoning and the ability to distil and synthesise complex data appear particularly effortless to barristers, underpinned by their sharp focus on attention to detail and ability to think quickly on their feet.

However, being methodical and systematic and adhering to rules and procedures often suffocate flexibility and creativity, suppressing the desire to change or to be more visionary and long-term focused when required; defaulting to tried-and-tested methods is more the modus operandi for this group.

Attending to the 'here and now' and the information to hand can stifle greater interest in the broader business arena and implications, not least when required to mitigate for risk. These practitioners are generally revered as trusted advisers and articulate communicators who are renowned for their integrity and knowledge; their presence is respected and professional credibility is assumed. However, as leaders of people within their own practice, they may come across as less open and empathetic, and as lacking the softer skills to support the growth and development of those they should inspire. Using competency frameworks to describe the behaviours will help define a clearer path to all-round success.

Once a competency framework has been established, it is likely that different levels of proficiency will be allocated to each one. The example set out in Table 4 opposite is from the Chartered Institute of Marketing (CIM).[102]

Interestingly, the CIM organises its Professional Marketing Competencies into three areas: core, technical and behaviour. The latter category relates mostly to soft skills and includes aspects such as creativity, influencing, collaboration, responsibility, financial literacy,

Table 4. Chartered Institute of Marketing proficiency levels

Level		Definition	Knowledge	Application
5	Authoritative	Mastery at the highest level of the knowledge and application	Mastery	Habitual
4	Accomplished	An advanced degree of knowledge and consistent application	Mastery	Regular
3	Able	Full knowledge of the concepts and application to the business	Full	Regular
2	Active learner	Meaningful knowledge with some experience and application	Some	Some
1	Aware	Limited knowledge or experience with full potential to develop	Limited	Limited

inspiration, innovation, challenges, entrepreneurial spirit and commercial awareness.

5. Measuring the effectiveness of training

Designing, developing and delivering soft skills training is one challenge. Measuring the effectiveness of that training is another.

Many training programmes rely on delegates self-reporting their own views of the effectiveness of the training. And there are many issues with this approach.

Most firms will look to the appraisal process or competency frameworks to see whether people are developing and exhibiting the required behaviours. A few firms have invested in technology solutions – such as Performance Leader – to monitor lawyer skills from the perspective of peers and clients.

The measurement of learning effectiveness is an area of expertise among educational and L&D professionals. And not all law firms have access to such resources.

So this means that measuring learning effectiveness remains difficult – and so deciding to invest in training programmes remains challenging.

Culture, commerciality, coaching and wellbeing

Victoria Heming has been the human resources director at Thomson Snell and Passmore – the country's oldest law firm, with 260 staff – for 15 years. She previously worked at AXA Investment Managers, Guardian Royal Exchange Group and EY.

We've just experienced a cultural lift when we moved everyone in our Tunbridge Wells offices from three old buildings into a brand-new, modern, open-plan office. The design and layout, café and break-out areas have released a huge amount of energy and, with the help of some working groups from across the firm, are helping to drive better internal communication and cross-selling.

We engender an understanding here that personal skills are not soft skills, but rather the hard, gritty skills that are needed – in addition to black-letter law skills – for lawyers to operate at their highest potential.

We run a lot of mainstream, informative, 'have-a-go' training programmes and know-how sessions – all of which are modular to suit different levels of experience – in small, 'bite-sized' pieces, such as introductory sessions and more advanced practice.

Commerciality skills

A current focus is on commerciality skills and law in business. Our lawyers, legal support and business services professionals need to understand how our business runs – vision and strategy, financial management, technology and people management – if they are to be effective leaders in the future. We have recently involved all staff in the development of our next five-year plan.

We also help them to develop their understanding of our clients and the commercial environments in which they operate. We want our people to work, think and behave in a commercial way, and to develop the gravitas, confidence and credibility needed for when they are in front of clients. We need to really 'get' our clients' business, culture and needs – we get this from qualitative and quantitative feedback received from clients. This training is inclusive and extended to our most junior lawyers and trainees.

Health and wellbeing skills

On the other side, we recently launched our health and wellbeing strategy and introduced the concept of building resilience into all aspects of our working lives. We are providing the tools for leaders and managers to help them create the right levels of stretch, manage stress and build resilience in their teams. But we are also starting this development work early with younger lawyers and support staff, so that it becomes part of the firm's DNA in the future.

Coaching support
We've also had real success with coaching and training our most senior people in strategy, leadership and wellbeing. The one-to-one coaching process – drawing on a range of external coaches with different skills, approaches and experiences, so that the chemistry match is good – provides reflective space and encourages senior lawyers to take care of themselves and others when juggling many responsibilities on different fronts to fulfil their contribution to the firm.

Measurement of training effectiveness
We use a variety of tools to measure training effectiveness. There are engagement surveys with detailed questions. We facilitate 'no holds barred' workshops with a mixture of seniorities to increase internal exposure and create a cultural feedback loop. We also monitor performance reviews and exit interviews, and reflect on what we can do differently and better.

We encourage reflection – to give the time, space and psychological safety – among all of our people, so that continuous self-development becomes a normal part of work life. And our investment in the L&D of our lawyers is integral with our investment in our legal support and business services staff.

6. Awards for soft skills development
At the March 2020 Managing Partners Forum Management Excellence Awards[103] in London, there were numerous law firm winners with an L&D focus, providing insight into what some of the leading law firms had achieved and how they had done so.

Dentons won the Best L&D Programme award for its suite of five interdependent leadership programmes aimed at developing high-performing associates and partners. The firm applies innovative research in neuroscience and EQ, with creative and modern learning options to transform how it thinks, leads and engages its diverse and multi-generational talent. Testimonials for the programmes showed effective learning, which was also reflected in quantitative measures of personal development.

PwC, the accountancy practice that also provides legal services, came second in this category. There was strategic alignment in the PwC programme from the engagement of new leaders and an open dialogue about the firm's strategic challenges. The design contemplated a range of learning styles and recognised the need to apply skills, reflect and refine. The programme has produced strong results, both quantitative and qualitative, particularly in relation to talent development. The impact of the programme on some participants could be described as transformational.

Runner-up in the Best Business Innovation category, White & Case has spread awareness of and engagement with its innovation activities through its LIFT programme in the London office, encouraging both understanding and cultural change. This involved both a live event showcasing some of the firm's practice technologies and a training academy to combine communication and training. The LIFT programme has created excitement and interest, and has positively impacted on employee engagement with innovation. Future events are planned within the London office, and similar programmes have been implemented or are planned in offices in Asia-Pacific, New York and Germany.

VI. The range of soft skills required by lawyers

We have seen there are several distinct skill sets required in law firms:

- technical legal skills;
- language skills;
- technology skills;
- leadership skills; and
- soft skills – emotional, communication and interpersonal skills.

There are also business skills, encapsulated in the relevant professional bodies of each functional area relating to management topics such as:

- strategy and planning;
- change management;
- finance;
- marketing;
- HR;
- real estate;
- risk management; and
- technology.

1. Essential soft skills for lawyers

Drawing on all the research undertaken in the development of this report, I have attempted to set out in Table 5 a definitive list of essential soft skills for lawyers. Some occur in more than one category, but I have only mentioned them once for simplicity. Business development skills are broken down into three categories: marketing, selling and relationship development.

Table 5. Essential soft skills for lawyers

Client care	• Client experience management • Complaints handling • Expectations management • Service delivery
Communication	• Active listening • Face-to-face communications and meetings • Online (emails, social media and videoconferencing) • Storytelling • Telephone (inbound and outbound) • Writing
Consulting	• Commerciality • Estimating and forecasting • Scoping • Pricing • Project management
Leadership	• Change management • Innovation • Inspiring • Planning • Stakeholder management • Visioning
Marketing	• Analysis and targeting • Campaign development • Client listening • Content creation (eg, written, podcasts, videos) • Differentiation • Thought leadership • Value proposition development
Personal effectiveness	• Assertiveness • Confidence • Decision making • Goal setting • Making an impact (personal branding) • Reflection

continued on next page

Personal effectiveness continued	• Self-awareness • Self-development (and learning) • Time management and prioritisation
Problem solving	• Analysis • Creativity • Critical thinking • Idea and option generation • Research • Solutions development
Relationships	• Adapting personal style • Appreciating diversity • Conflict management • Cross-cultural competency • Empathy and EQ • Influence • Mediation • Negotiation • Rapport building • Referrer management • Social proficiency • Trust building
Selling	• Account management • Adding value and insight • Cross-selling • Identifying needs, opportunities and threats • Listening • Networking – face to face and on social media • Persuasion • Pitching and tendering • Presenting and performance • Questioning
Team management	• Coaching • Delegation • Facilitation • Feedback • Mentoring • Motivating • Performance management • Supervision • Training and development

2. Lawyer qualities and attributes

Something that was frequently mentioned during the research interviews was the idea that lawyers need certain key qualities or attributes. Some of the most common qualities that good lawyers need include the following:

- adaptability;
- authenticity;
- calmness;
- collaboration;
- commerciality;
- compassion;
- confidence;
- courage;
- creativity;
- curiosity;
- decisiveness;
- determination;
- empathy;
- energy;
- enthusiasm;
- fairness;
- gravitas;
- humility;
- intuitiveness;
- judgement;
- motivation;
- openness;
- optimism;
- patience;
- positivity;
- predictability;
- proactivity;
- professionalism;
- respectfulness;
- responsiveness;
- versatility; and
- wisdom.

In 2019 QDooz[104] completed research – in conjunction with Britain Thinks – gauging the views of 1,000 UK adults and more than 100 UK decision makers to develop the National Qualities Index (NQI). The results are set out in Table 6 opposite.

Table 6. National Qualities Index (QDooz with Britain Thinks)

1 Reliable	22 Strategic	43 Grounded	64 Harmonious
2 Efficient	23 Involved	44 Friendly	65 Curious
3 Adaptable	24 Purposeful	45 Authentic	66 Discerning
4 Organised	25 Persevering	46 Visionary	67 Easy-going
5 Committed	26 Intuitive	47 Wise	68 Forgiving
6 Responsible	27 Understanding	48 Loyal	69 Generous
7 Focused	28 Encouraging	49 Optimistic	70 Gracious
8 Consistent	29 Perceptive	50 Courteous	71 Adventurous
9 Confident	30 Fair	51 Compassionate	72 Unique
10 Honest	31 Analytical	52 Energetic	73 Idealistic
11 Collaborative	32 Assertive	53 Empathetic	74 Humble
12 Achieving	33 Patient	54 Entrepreneurial	75 Grateful
13 Disciplined	34 Calm	55 Independent	76 Sensitive
14 Practical	35 Creative	56 Healthy	77 Humorous
15 Decisive	36 Future-focused	57 Relational	78 Traditional
16 Resilient	37 Excellent	58 Caring	79 Detached
17 Respectful	38 Sincere	59 Competitive	80 Loving
18 Open-minded	39 Self-assured	60 Safe	81 Vulnerable
19 Listening	40 Influential	61 Kind	
20 Accountable	41 Trusting	62 Expressive	
21 Enthusiastic	42 Self-aware	63 Courageous	

VII. Five essential soft skills for lawyers

Hopefully, this report has provided some insight into the wide variety of soft skills required by lawyers.

In the preceding chapters, EQ emerged as a critical feature of many personal and interpersonal skills for lawyers. It is not possible to address all of the required soft skills in one report. So in this section, I have selected five soft skill areas – personal, communication, building relationships, leadership and business development – and provided some introductory materials on three elements of each.

1. Personal skills

There are many personal skills needed by lawyers, much of which are underpinned by EQ. Here I have selected goal setting, personal impact and creativity for further consideration.

1.1 Goal setting

Goal setting is an essential behaviour for a wide range of activities, including time management, organisation, resource allocation, team management, leadership, motivation, coaching, problem-solving, negotiation, performance management, resilience, business development and change management.

(a) Prioritisation and self-management

In law firms, it is usual to have many conflicting demands on time; so the ability to constantly revise goals in the light of new information is important.

Too often, urgent pressures (eg, client demands, fee-earning targets) overshadow important matters such as talent development and marketing, unless a disciplined approach is taken to continually monitor short, medium and long-term goals.

The economic model of behaviour suggests that we make rational decisions based on our goals. However, neuroscience suggests a different hypothesis: we make comparisons between ourselves now and ourselves in the future, thinking about our future self as though he or she were another person.

The *Harvard Business Review* recently reported[105] that at many companies, people spend around 80% of their time in meetings or answering colleagues' requests, leaving little time for all the critical work they must complete on their own. This is called 'collaborative overload' and senior management teams must be aware of this problem and strive to mitigate it.

"Too often, urgent pressures (eg, client demands, fee-earning targets) overshadow important matters such as talent development and marketing, unless a disciplined approach is taken to continually monitor short, medium and long-term goals."

(b) Lawyer targets and short-termism
Often, lawyers are given personal fee-earning targets that concentrate their minds on the short term. This can result in a focus on inputs (ie, time recorded and fees) rather than outputs and results (ie, client satisfaction and profit). Efficiency can become more important than effectiveness.

There's a famous saying that "Turnover is vanity; profit is sanity; but cash flow is king." Many have observed that lawyers tend to focus their attention on generating fees, when they should instead be considering profits and cash flow.

Without consideration of medium and longer-term goals, it is easy for lawyers to experience strategic drift – building a client base and practice that reflect a reactive response to demands, rather than a proactive attempt to attract the desired types of clients and instructions.

(c) Leadership and strategic thinking

> *Alice: Would you tell me, please, which way I ought to go from here?*
> *The Cheshire Cat: That depends a good deal on where you want to get to.*
> *Alice: I don't much care where.*
> *The Cheshire Cat: Then it doesn't much matter which way you go*
> Lewis Carroll[106]

The essence of strategic thinking is to consider your current position and where you want to be in the future, so that you can select the best course of action to achieve your goals. To achieve engagement and implementation, leaders must ensure that the firm's goals align and integrate with those of its offices, teams and individuals.

Most people will be familiar with the need to set specific, measureable, achievable, realistic and time-specific (SMART) objectives. But sometimes this can be difficult, especially if the goals are hard to measure (eg, reputation) or the aims are too general.

(d) Visualisation and scenarios
In *The New One Minute Manager*,[107] Ken Blanchard and Spencer Johnson suggest the following goal-setting approach:

- Agree on your goals.
- Think about what good behaviour looks like.
- Write out each of your goals on a single sheet of paper, using fewer than 250 words.
- Read and re-read your goal, which takes only a minute or so each time.

> *"The stepping-stone approach may prove useful to lawyers. This involves identifying a long-term goal and then working backwards to see what must be done each month, quarter or year in order to move towards achieving it."*

- Take a minute out of your day every once in a while to look at your performance.
- See whether your behaviour matches your goal.

Many years later, psychologists studying performance discovered that high-achieving individuals routinely practise two 'prepping' habits:

- They form clear mental pictures of what they want to achieve; and
- They write down descriptions of those achieved states.

Neurological researchers have not yet determined why there is a correlation between these habits and success – but there is nonetheless a scientific consensus that it exists.

Where there is a lot of uncertainty – such as in today's volatile, uncertain, complex and ambiguous (VUCA) world – it may be more appropriate to use scenario analyses rather than goal-setting techniques. Allen & Overy adopted scenario analysis many years ago.[108]

(e) Stepping-stone approach

The stepping-stone approach may prove useful to lawyers. This involves identifying a long-term goal and then working backwards to see what must be done each month, quarter or year in order to move towards achieving it.

It is also helpful to break things down. For example, to achieve £1 million in fees what is the optimal mix of matters of different value: 10 cases at £100,000 or 100 cases at £10,000?

Similarly, you can start by thinking about how many enquiries you need to generate or contacts to make in order to convert these into the requisite number of client cases. In business development, we call this the 'sales pipeline' – for example, we might learn that 100 enquiries generate 30 conversations, which subsequently generate 10 proposals and three instructions.

(f) Project management and KPIs

More sophisticated firms will have firm, department, office and individual goals across a range of factors, such as finance, clients, people and business development. These goals may be put into operation through project management processes that allocate milestones and KPIs along the way.

Increasingly, firms are using technology to track lawyers' progress against a variety of client, team and financial goals. Management information systems then present these KPIs as dashboards, so that it is easy to manage performance and identify outliers of under or over-performance.

Some law firms use the Performance Leader system to track KPIs for individuals, teams and the whole firm across a range of financial, client satisfaction and HR measures.

(g) Motivation and coaching

Motivation is the passion to work for internal reasons that go beyond money and status. Motivation is driven by an inner vision of what is important in life, the joy of doing something, curiosity to learn, immersion in an activity and the energetic and persistent pursuit of goals.

Goal setting is an essential part of the coaching and development process. The latest research by Richard Boyatzis, Melvin Smith and Ellen Van Oosten on compassionate coaching argues that the first step is always to identify the ideal self and personal vision: "To make changes stick, our research shows that it has to be intentionally and internally motivated rather than imposed from the outside."[109]

Years ago, Locke's goal-setting research[110] found that:

- difficult goals lead to higher performance than easy goals;
- specific goals lead to higher performance than general goals; and
- knowledge of results (feedback) is essential.

(h) Mental wellbeing

Psychologists have found that goals are integral to wellbeing. The three core elements of wellbeing are emotions, engagement and meaning. Six additional features are self-esteem, optimism, resilience, vitality, self-determination and positive relationships. Some argue that this model is insufficient without accomplishment. In his brilliant book *Lost Connections*,[111] Johann Hari suggests that disconnection from meaningful work is one of the nine causes of depression.

David Rock and Dan Siegal[112] found that focusing time on goal-oriented activities is one of the seven essential daily mental activities for optimum brain health. People will experience stress if they have goals that are either unachievable or too easy to achieve.

Psychologist Gabriele Oettingen found that people generally adopt one of three goal-setting strategies:

"Focusing time on goal-oriented activities is one of the seven essential daily mental activities for optimum brain health. People will experience stress if they have goals that are either unachievable or too easy to achieve."

- Optimists envision the future they hope to achieve and its benefits.
- Pessimists think of all the obstacles that will prevent them from achieving this future.
- Those who employ 'mental contrasting' combine both strategies by comparing a positive outcome and simultaneously concentrating on the obstacles in the way. Only the mental contrasting method is correlated with actual achievement.

The latest research supports Oettingen's WOOP method (Wish, Outcome, Obstacle, Plan): "by fooling our brains into thinking we are already successful, we lose motivation and energy to do what it takes to actually become successful".[113]

For more on mental wellbeing and stress management, see p 37.

1.2 Making an impact, messaging and personal brand

(a) Making an impact
To achieve success, both internally and externally, lawyers need to make a personal impact.

The ability to make an impact depends on a variety of factors, including physical appearance, personality, presence, verbal communication and non-verbal communication (NVC), energy, confidence and behaviour.

The API model developed by Peter Hawkins[114] recognises the importance of:

- authority (expertise);
- presence (attractiveness); and
- impact (the ability to create change by asking incisive questions).

The PVI model instead focuses on perception, visibility and influence.[115] Both confirm that in order to make an impact, lawyers need to stand out (in the right way), speak up and make a difference.

(b) Messaging
The starting point to make an impact is to identify the three key messages that you would like people to remember that make you different; that make you stand out from the crowd.

These three key messages should form the basis of the information you include in social media and web profiles, introductions at networking events and content shared on digital channels. By

"Lawyers in larger firms often leverage the firm's brand, whereas those in smaller firms tend to build their own personal brand. In the best cases, lawyers use both."

reinforcing these key messages in everything that they say and do, lawyers can become memorable.

Too often, lawyers describe themselves in general terms or attempt to present themselves as 'good at everything', which makes it more difficult for people to remember them when considering, choosing or recommending an adviser.

One method I use to help lawyers develop their messaging is the 3×3 matrix:

- "I work with..." (three types of clients);
- "My background is..." (three areas of expertise or types of work); and
- "I help clients by..." (three types of solution or benefits).

(c) Personal brand

In order to raise their profile, lawyers also need to develop their own personal brand.

Lawyers in larger firms often leverage the firm's brand, whereas those in smaller firms tend to build their own personal brand. In the best cases, lawyers use both.

In his book on building a personal brand, Daniel Priestley[116] described how to decommoditise your personal brand and shift from functionality to vitality using the SALT process:

- social footprint;
- awards and associations;
- live appearances; and
- third-party media mentions.

1.3 Creativity

Creativity is an essential part of complex problem-solving behaviour and was mentioned many times during the research interviews for this special report. It is also one of the areas where lawyers can 'robot-proof' themselves from the march of automation.

The need to develop complex problem-solving skills

Ray D'Cruz is a former lawyer based in Australia who is now the founder and CEO of Performance Leader. Performance Leader produces agile software through which clients can provide instant feedback on work and lawyers, allowing practice leaders to manage and develop high-performance staff more effectively and efficiently.

I am really interested in the area of complex problem solving – particularly in view of the direction that the legal market is moving, with the rise of automation and AI. It is here that the lawyers of the future can really add value for clients and remain relevant.

We've been collaborating with Australia's leading law firm strategy consultant, Joel Barolsky, to develop the concept of 'the profoundly human law firm of 2030'. In the medium and large commercial law firms of the future, lawyers will need to leverage the deeply human abilities of creativity, problem solving and collaboration.

The best lawyers have always been extremely creative; but perhaps that has been an unconscious competency, and therefore has not been articulated and transferred. There needs to be more conscious awareness of its value and how it is developed. This is a great opportunity for firms to engage their most creative people. Over the years, so many talented young people from diverse backgrounds with creative skills either didn't make it into law firms or were placed into narrow types of work and never got to express this capability – and subsequently left the profession.

Where we once highlighted 'judgement' as one of the dividing lines between partners and non-partners, largely based on managing legal risk, the dividing line between future leaders and others might be complex problem-solving capability. Judgement infers that the knowledge and wisdom are self-contained; whereas problem solving allows for the answers to client challenges to be found beyond one person. It means collaboration across practice groups and allows for external networks beyond the firm to be deployed for the benefit of clients. Future leaders will bring their whole network – internal and external – to bear for the benefit of the client.

That will also mean being able to lead diverse teams. We know diverse teams are better at solving complex problems. For the leader, this means understanding and deploying the full breadth of diversity – and not just the diversity we see, but also diversity of thought and neuro-diversity.

Training in many firms is hopeless – it is so slow and arbitrary. The consequence is that many law firms don't trust non-partners to lead client relationships, preferring to make expensive and often poor lateral partner hires rather than help junior staff step up. Contrast that to other sectors. One of Melbourne's best restaurants has just appointed a 24-year-old head chef, to provide creative direction and lead a large team. What kind of rapid development process enables an appointment like this? Nothing like what you see in most law firms.

The US Air Force – as described in the book The Debrief Imperative[117] *– uses intense, rapid and agile feedback to prepare 25-year-old pilots to fly $35 million planes. Every mission is followed by a structured debrief. In the same way, high-performance sports teams review every game to identify what worked and what didn't, and discuss how to change things next time. The same teams even undertake these reviews mid-game so that they can make adjustments before it's too late. Would you follow a sports team that waited six months or a year to review its performance?*

We're implementing our performance and feedback software with an Australian firm that is committed to before-action reviews (clarifying objectives and anticipating challenges at the start of the matter), mid-action reviews and after-action reviews. This serious and progressive approach makes it an outlier. Research we conducted with the Managing Partners Forum showed that fewer than 15% of law firms hold routine, structured debriefs at the end of matters. Even fewer conduct mid-matter reviews and matter previews. The flipside of this state is there is an opportunity for law firms that want to get serious about building a high-performance culture to make this a point of differentiation.

There are many definitions of 'creativity', but I like this one from Dr Jane Henry of the Open Business School,[118] which I came across during my MBA studies in the 1990s: "The quality of originality that leads to new ways of seeing and novel ideas. It is a thinking process associated with imagination, insight, invention, ingenuity, inspiration and illumination." Henry saw the essential ingredients of creativity as positivity, playfulness, passion/purpose and persistence.

(a) Curiosity

Curiosity is the desire to acquire new knowledge and experiences. Curious people explore, research and ask lots of questions, so they are often skilled at relationship management and selling.

Psychologists recognise two types of curiosity – individual trait curiosity and situational curiosity. Curiosity has a strong genetic element – some studies show that this accounts for between 45% and 61% of the variance.[119]

(b) Mental models and narrow ways of thinking

A mental model is an explanation of one's thought process about how something works in the real world. It is a representation of the surrounding world, the relationships between its parts and a person's intuitive perception of his or her own acts and their consequences.

Each of us has our own mental model, created through our interpretations of our experiences. However, we develop similar mental models when we work closely with those in the same environment. It may thus be argued that those who have only ever worked in legal private practice will have very similar mental models and thought processes.

You need to possess a wider repertoire of mental models and the expert intuition to select the right models to be creative. You also need to be able to recognise and manage structural biases in your own thinking, which means asking others to test out and scrutinise your ideas.

(c) Psychometric tests for creativity

Psychometric tests can identify traits that are indicative of greater creativity. For example, the British Psychological Society's NEO[120] identifies the 'Big Five' personality constructs of neuroticism, extraversion, agreeableness, competence and openness. It is this last factor – openness – which is thought to be an indicator of creativity.

The Herrmann Brain Dominance Instrument (HBDI)[121] provides insight into whether people are right brain or left brain dominant. If you are mostly analytical and methodical in your thinking, you are said to be left-brained. If you tend to be more creative or artistic, you are thought to be right-brained.

The Kirton Adaption-Innovation Inventory assessment[122] considers how cognitive style can impact on creativity and whether this is focused on adapting to or breaking the 'rules'. Lawyers generally tend to be adapters rather than innovators.

Dr Robert Epstein, a psychologist at Harvard, is a leading thinker on creativity. He developed a simple model which identified the following important dimensions of creativity (creative competencies):[123]

- Capturing: This relates to how well you capture and preserve ideas as they occur to you.
- Challenging: Challenges and failures help to stimulate new ideas through a process Epstein calls 'resurgence'. This competency is also helpful in dealing with stress.
- Broadening: By expanding your skills and knowledge base, as previously established, ideas compete and become interconnected. Learning new things supports creativity – and the further from your current areas of knowledge and expertise, the better. In intelligence and ability tests, this often relates to intellectual curiosity.
- Surrounding: Epstein's research shows that creativity is stimulated when people are exposed to novel or ambiguous stimuli. He suggests that you should deliberately manipulate both your physical and social environments on a regular basis.

(d) Creativity needs more than personality

But creativity needs more than personality – many suggest that it also relies on process and place (environment).

In her book *Time to Think*,[124] psychologist Nancy Kline outlined the 10 components of a thinking environment and demonstrated that the male conditioning in many Western cultures represents the very opposite of these.

(e) Developing creativity

Arthur Van Gundy[125] broke down the problem-solving process as follows:

- pre-problem solving;
- problem definition and analysis (including boundary examination);
- idea generation;
- evaluation and selection of ideas; and
- implementation.

A wide range of tools is available in each area. For example, for idea generation, there are techniques to support both divergent and convergent thinking, such as analogies and metaphors, forced association, superheroes, perspectives, storyboards and De Bono's thinking hats.[126]

Several firms have also started working with design thinking. Ideo, a global design and innovation company, says:

> *Design thinking is a process for creative problem-solving. It has a human-centered core. It encourages organizations to focus on the people they're creating, which leads to better products, services, and internal processes. When you sit down to create a solution for a business need, the first question should always be 'what's the human need behind it?' In employing design thinking, you're pulling together what's desirable from a human point of view with what is technologically feasible and economically viable. It also allows those who aren't trained as designers to use creative tools to address a vast range of challenges. The process starts with taking action and understanding the right questions. It's about embracing simple mind-set shifts and tackling problems from a new direction.*[127]

There is also considerable debate about the importance of the collection and assessment of facts in the early stages of the legal process.

2. Communication skills

Communication is the lifeblood of relationships. Lawyers communicate in just about every aspect of their work – whether collaborating with colleagues, leading teams, managing client expectations or pitching for new business.

Many of the soft skills mentioned in the research interviews for this special report alluded to communication. And these skills will vary depending on the medium being used – for example:

- writing skills for non-technical drafting, such as in day-to-day client emails, prose in marketing applications and persuasive writing in pitch documents;
- telephone skills for responding to client requests, participating in conference calls and following up contacts; and
- face-to-face communication skills with one or a number of individuals – in both formal and informal situations, in established and new relationships, in real or virtual teams, and in collaborative and conflict situations

A whole host of communication topics are mentioned throughout the research in this report and it would be impossible to address all of them in detail. I have therefore selected the three which I consider to be most important: NVC, active listening and storytelling.

Client communication skills

Jo Maude is a project manager and trainer who has worked in the creative industries since 1985. I worked with her on a skills framework for creative people at Design and Art Direction – the global association for the creative industries – many years ago. Her thoughts about the skills of creative people who sell their ideas and knowledge also ring true for many lawyers.

I think the main issue is around communication. Creative people – like lawyers – can be quite insular. They have brilliant ideas, but sometimes fail to articulate and explain those ideas to clients. They need to read people, politics and situations, and adapt accordingly – whether it is what they say or the tone of voice used. Empathy is the vital skill here. Often they fail to engage with the client – there's no conversation – so they are unable to collaborate.

Collaboration within a long-term relationship is critical. It is needed to develop the best solution for the client. And you have to be open and honest and trust each other. Of course, you need to have a clear process for projects. But sometimes you need time where there is no agenda and you can take in the bigger picture and the way that the relationship and work is going.

Sometimes you need to step back and spend half an hour over coffee offering each other feedback and critiques. You can't be precious– your job is to find the best solution together.

Storytelling skills are very important. You need to take clients on a journey – through your thought processes from the brief or problem to a solution. You mustn't be afraid to ask questions with confidence, but you need to avoid asking too many – achieving that balance is a real skill.

And you always need to do more than is expected – to make that extra effort. Younger team members can offer help in small ways or take the initiative and make themselves invaluable.

When it comes to design thinking – where you take in the entire user experience – you need to think about the client and their clients, and see things from their perspective. This means going beyond rehearsing for important pitch presentations to think about what happens when the client arrives at your offices, as he or she walks around your building and enters the meeting room.

You also need to learn from mistakes. Take something positive from any situations that don't go so well. If you fall off a horse, you get right back on it. You need to embrace the situation and learn for the future. Team learning is important – but that doesn't work in a blame culture.

2.1 Non-verbal communication

Many argue that how you say things is more important than what you say. Albert Mehrabian's findings[128] on how meaning in initial encounters is communicated are often quoted: 7% by the spoken word, 38% by the voice and 55% by other non-verbal cues, including appearance, posture and gestures. I refer to these as 'words', 'music' and 'dance'. The importance of visual cues is perhaps less surprising when we consider the eye has 18 times more neurons than the ear – we have greater bandwidth for visual information than for auditory information.

More recently, Alex Pentland of Massachusetts Institute of Technology[129] proved that people are dramatically influenced by non-verbal signals. He found that consistency in tone and motion indicates

"The importance of visual cues is perhaps less surprising when we consider the eye has 18 times more neurons than the ear – we have greater bandwidth for visual information than for auditory information."

that someone knows what he or she is doing. He showed that when pitching, you can estimate ratings purely by tone of voice; and that you can measure the effectiveness of leaders without hearing what they are saying. You can predict a leader's success at certain tasks by observing his or her NVC. He also learned that the most successful people are more energetic, talk more, listen more and spend more time face to face with people.

When interpreting NVC, it is important to be aware of culture and context. There is a huge variety in NVC across nations, so there is plenty of scope for misinterpretation. There are regional variations, too – for example, those from urban areas differ in their NVC from those from rural spaces. It is advisable to consider clusters of gestures, rather than focusing on an isolated movement.

It seems that many people could benefit from a deeper understanding of the impact of NVC at the moment, judging by performances on teleconference calls and virtual meetings during the coronavirus lockdown. NVC is a critical element of your digital and online presence.

(a) Creating a great first impression

You only have one chance to make a first impression
Stephanie Perkins[130]

It only takes a fraction of a second for people to form a first impression, so this is typically formed by non-verbal signals. Evidence suggests that it is unlikely that an initial impression will change.

(b) Eye contact and smiling

In Western cultures, eye contact and smiling are important when making contact. Changes in eye contact are often perceived negatively. When speaking to a group of people, you increase everyone's sense of involvement by 'light-housing' – sweeping your eye contact periodically around all the individuals present.

(c) Voice and confidence

Those with lower-pitched and louder voices, and those who speak quickly, are perceived more positively than those with high-pitched, softer voices or who speak slowly.

People assume that louder voices convey greater confidence and authority, and that speed of speech reflects on intelligence (but also nervousness, if speech is too rapid). Research also shows that some accents are received much more favourably than others. Although it is difficult to change how you speak, an awareness of this will help you to understand how other people will perceive you.

"It only takes a fraction of a second for people to form a first impression, so this is typically formed by non-verbal signals. Evidence suggests that it is unlikely that an initial impression will change."

Another cue for confidence is the amount of space you use – those who dominate the space and adopt an open posture are seen as more confident than those who occupy a small space and cross their arms and legs. The work of psychologist Amy Cuddy[131] is interesting – she showed that adopting one of five power poses (which typically involve dominating space) for just two minutes increases your testosterone levels, which makes you feel more confident. This is a case of 'fake it 'til you make it' in action.

With your voice, you can convey personality, passion and personal commitment by taking care with your projection (volume), pitch, pace, pauses and prosody.

(d) Mirroring and rapport

If someone's NVC mirrors or matches your own, then it may be an indication that he or she feels a degree of rapport with you. Neuro-linguistic programming (NLP) – a form of applied psychology – advises people to observe and subtly match or mirror the other person's NVC in order to accelerate the process. Alex Pentland found that this relates to the mirror neuron system – when people mimic gestures, this is correlated to feelings of empathy and trust.

(e) Buying signals

NVC is a powerful tool in selling situations. If people suddenly sit forward or tilt their heads as if to listen more intently in meetings, they may be sending buying signals. People will also sit forward when they wish to speak and will try to pick up the eye contact 'baton' to take over the conversation.

Similarly, if people sit back or fold their arms, they may be resistant to your ideas or you may have lost their attention and interest. Glazed eyes, yawning and a head resting on a hand are other indications of disinterest. Displacement activity (eg, jiggling coins in a pocket) may indicate a suppressed desire to remove oneself from the situation or signal impatience or anxiety.

2.2 Active listening

> *Most people do not listen with the intent to understand. Most people listen with the intent to reply.*
> Stephen R Covey[132]

NVC plays a significant role in active listening. For example, maintaining steady eye contact (without staring) signals that you are engaging with the speaker. Mirroring or matching the other person's posture, breathing and gestures can signal rapport. Nods and smiles encourage people to continue. Watching for inconsistencies between what someone is saying and his or her NVC may provide insight into their true feelings. They present opportunities to explore contradictions.

It is said that great salespeople spend a great deal of time listening rather than talking. They listen actively, using energy to show that they are paying attention, respecting the speaker and encouraging the speaker to continue. People often need time to think and reflect on a question or point before offering a response. Showing your tolerance for a comfortable silence gives others time to explore and articulate their feelings and thoughts.

Active listening is a skill. It takes effort, concentration and empathy. Research shows that we remember less than 10% of what people tell us. There are many techniques to improve our listening skills. For example, paraphrasing or saying what the other person has said in your own words demonstrates that you are absorbing the information and understand the essence of his or her communication. It offers an opportunity for the other person to reflect on how his or her words are being perceived and correct the emphasis or meaning if necessary.

People are more likely to be receptive to what you have to say if they have had the chance to express all their thoughts on the matter. By highlighting the important issues first, you can help them to feel heard and validated. Simply repeating back or reflecting words and phrases confirms that you are listening and encourages further dialogue. It helps to build trust, in allowing that person to continue to speak without fear of you making (premature) judgements.

When you develop an opinion, preconception or hypothesis about someone – for example, labelling him or her as 'difficult' – your brain filters out all the information that contradicts your theory, so you miss it to avoid cognitive dissonance. You only hear the information that confirms your initial belief. Exploring your pre-conceptions, assumptions and biases can help you to listen more openly.

Effective selling means paying attention to what is being said and how it is being said. In a sales situation, the more information the other person has provided, the more likely it is that you will identify some trigger, angle, need or opportunity that you can explore to make your pitch more relevant and resonant.

Psychologists use listening inventories and listening preference profiles to understand our approach to listening.

"Great salespeople spend a great deal of time listening rather than talking. They listen actively, using energy to show that they are paying attention, respecting the speaker and encouraging the speaker to continue."

"In a sales situation, the more information the other person has provided, the more likely it is that you will identify some trigger, angle, need or opportunity that you can explore to make your pitch more relevant and resonant."

Business development skills – listening, lateral thinking and planning

Denise Kitchener is head of business development at Osbornes Law. Previously, she spent nearly 20 years as CEO at the Association of Personal Injury Lawyers and worked at Pattinson & Brewer, Hodge Jones & Allen, Hudgell Solicitors and 187 Fleet Street Chambers.

> *There are a whole range of soft skills needed by lawyers, but those which are of most interest to me are interpersonal, communication, teamwork, negotiation, adaptation, problem solving, creativity and time management.*
>
> *There is a particular issue with listening skills. I wonder whether it is because litigators like to analyse things and take control, whereas when you listen you are allowing the other person to lead the conversation. When lawyers are networking, they need to learn to stand back, listen and learn. With this approach, they may learn about situations where the client has an issue – even if it isn't in their immediate area of expertise.*
>
> *Another issue is around lateral thinking. Some lawyers can be rather narrow in their thinking, focusing primarily on what they do themselves rather than understanding and being aware of the abilities of their colleagues in other parts of the firm. Once they have mastered their own 60-second elevator pitch, they need to help develop similar pitches for their colleagues – in private client or employment teams, for example. They need to consider how they can help the client from a firm perspective as well as individually.*
>
> *In business development, we need to be aware that lawyers have different personalities and a range of abilities. I encourage lawyers to celebrate their strengths rather than worrying about their limitations. Not all lawyers might be good at writing crisp marketing copy, but they may be brilliant at presenting. Similarly, other lawyers may be at their best in a one-to-one situation with prospects and clients. So there needs to be a team approach to tackling the range of business development activities.*
>
> *It's not exactly a soft skill, but more an attitude challenge. I have found that millennials are often really focused on what they are doing in the moment and can look surprised when asked about their future career plans. Work demands can often mean that they have not taken time to consider their personal plan or how they would like to specialise and position themselves in the future – which makes building a strong reputation for them difficult.*

I have observed that lawyers are least comfortable in learning environments that involve role play – they don't enjoy it. Workshops where they get to work together in groups seem preferable and more effective. Personally, I like training that really motivates and inspires me. I once attended a three-day course with Tony Robbins with 5,000 other people where I ended up walking on hot coals. It was a brilliant illustration that you can learn to do what seems impossible if you have the right mind-set.

2.3 Storytelling

One of the oldest forms of communication is storytelling. In times before the written word, storytelling (narrative reasoning) helped to pass on learning and values among tribes. Jennifer Aaker of Stanford Graduate School of Business[133] has revealed that stories are 22 times more memorable than facts. Another experiment found that while just 5% of people remembered a statistic, 64% remembered a story.

The human brain does not distinguish between reading or hearing a story and experiencing it in real life – the same neurological regions are activated. Stories activate parts of the brain that allow listeners to connect the story to their ideas and experience as a result of a process known as neural coupling.

"When you have to convey complexity, keep it simple: automatically adjust to the listener's level of knowledge and tailor the content to be more meaningful to him or her."

(a) Use empathy and adjust to the audience

> *People will forget what you said, people will forget what you did, but people will never forget how you made them feel.*
> Maya Angelou

When we think about the most memorable and inspiring speakers that we have heard, we often recollect their emotion and passion in delivery, rather than the actual content.

One reason why storytelling is so powerful is because it creates an emotional connection between the storyteller and the listener. You need empathy to be able to see things from the listener's point of view and craft your story so that it resonates with him or her.

(b) Keep it simple

> *Any fool can make things more complex; it takes a touch of genius to move in the opposite direction.*
> Albert Einstein

Our short-term memory can generally handle chunks of about seven pieces of information.[134] People find it easiest to retain three key pieces of information. Use this insight to include three key messages in your story that you want the audience to retain.

When you have to convey complexity, keep it simple: automatically adjust to the listener's level of knowledge and tailor the content to be more meaningful to him or her. Even TED talks on the most advanced scientific topics start with a simple idea and build up layers of complexity from there.

(c) Story essentials

You can develop your storytelling skills by understanding how stories are structured.

There are seven basic story plots:[135] overcoming the monster; the quest; journey and return; comedy; tragedy; rebirth; and rags to riches. There are likewise seven basic story elements: a hero; the hero's character flaw; enabling circumstances; the hero's ally; an opponent; a life-changing event; and jeopardy. Many of these elements can be seen in legal case studies and client testimonials.

Good stories follow a dramatic curve. They build tension to a conclusion and climax. Storybooks are often organised so that each chapter or section follows its own dramatic curve, so that you are drawn onto the next part of the story.

(d) Content and delivery

You must consider both the content of the story and its delivery.

Use the journalist's inverted pyramid[136] to convey the content as a one-sentence story. Be clear about the aims of your story – what you want people to feel and think and do as a result.

Think carefully about the words that you use. Use words that paint strong mental images. Use powerful words that evoke emotion. Adapt to the language of the people you are talking to.

Your NVC – in particular, your voice – will have an impact on how you deliver your story. So use it to good effect and allow your emotion to show in your face, your voice and your gestures. You will appear sincere and authentic if your NVC is congruent with your content.

(e) Hooks and bridges

A hook grabs people's attention. A bridge acts as a connection between something that the listener already knows and something that you are trying to explain. The Celtic cross is a good example of a bridge. The people of Ireland originally regarded the sun as an all-powerful force. The early Christians linked their story to that of the sun, which is why the Celtic cross combines the circle shape of the sun and the cross.

We also use analogies and metaphors to connect new information to ideas that people already know and understand. We connect to their existing frameworks of knowledge in their mental map of the world.

> *The greatest art in the world is the art of storytelling.*
> Cecil B DeMille
>
> *Marketing is no longer about the stuff that you make, but about the stories you tell.*
> Seth Godin
>
> *The most powerful person in the world is the storyteller. The storyteller sets the vision, values and agenda of an entire generation that is to come.*
> Steve Jobs

(f) Lawyers using stories

Lawyers can improve their communication effectiveness when presenting, networking, building client relationships and cross-selling by using stories.

Templates can be provided to help lawyers think about the best stories to express what they do, how they do it and the value they bring to clients.

Lawyers might need help with stepping back from the technical details to see the bigger picture of the client, its problems and what has happened in a particular scenario. A skilled interviewer – for example, someone trained in media relations – can help uncover great stories from lawyers and craft them into persuasive communications, whether written or spoken. Video is an effective way to share legal stories through digital and social media channels.

3. Building relationships

Building relationships is fundamental to just about everything that lawyers do. Right from the start of their legal careers, they must forge strong relationships with peers, colleagues, supervisors and leaders. They must quickly establish productive relationships with clients.

Some firms encourage young solicitors to start developing their network among peers both within and beyond the firm from the outset. In some firms, networking skills training is provided to trainees within the first few weeks of employment.

"Lawyers in global firms also need to extend their network internationally, across physical and psychological boundaries. This added complexity can test even the most experienced lawyers as they grapple with technological, geographical, chronological and cultural challenges."

Lawyers in global firms also need to extend their network internationally, across physical and psychological boundaries. This added complexity can test even the most experienced lawyers as they grapple with technological, geographical, chronological and cultural challenges.

3.1 A model of business relationships

In my book *Better Business Relationships: Insights from Psychology and Management for Working in a Digital World*,[137] I developed the DACRIE© model to explain the building blocks of relationship management:

- Difference and diversity – understanding yourself and other people:
  - personality, style, perception and cognition;
  - managing emotions, authenticity, EQ and empathy (see p 27); and
  - gender, generational and cultural differences.

- Adaptation and change:
  - habits, filters and comfort zones;
  - learning processes – managing change in ourselves and others (see p 63), and
  - resilience and stress management (see p 37).

- Communication:
  - face-to-face, telephone, presentation, written and digital communication (see p 93);
  - NVC (see p 95); and
  - influence, persuasion and storytelling (see p 102).

- Relationships and conflict management:
  - relationship management competencies, including rapport and trust;
  - different types of relationships and how they are formed; and
  - difficult behaviours, conflict management and negotiation (see p122).

- Internal relationships:
  - organisational culture, working with your manager and internal politics;
  - groups and teams – styles, integration, buy-in and performance; and
  - delegation, coaching, feedback, motivation and leadership.

- External relationships:
  - self-esteem, confidence and client service;

- decision-making processes – selling yourself and your ideas; and
- meetings, pitches, key accounts and referrer management.

Some of these topics are touched on in other parts of this report.

3.2 Understanding different types of relationships and how they are formed

Evidence shows that humans are motivated both to form bonds with one another (to receive affection and create a sense of belonging) and to carve out space for themselves (to achieve an individual identity and freedom). Researcher Leslie Baxter has developed a model of these opposing motivations, which create relational dialectics.[138] People manage these by moving closer or further away at different times in a relationship and we are rarely in sync, which can cause conflict.

There are various models that illustrate the stages of relationship formation. And you can often see these in evidence in the sales and client relationship management models that law firms adopt in their business development.

Martin Knapp[139] proposed the idea of relationship stages:

- initiation;
- experimentation;
- intensification;
- integration; and
- bonding.

You could consider the strength of the relationship as a progression:

- formation – getting to know each other;
- divergence – having differing opinions, with doubt and disagreement (moving apart);
- convergence – reconciliation, acceptance and agreement (coming together); and
- association – working together cooperatively or collaboratively.

Another pragmatic model offers the following stages of a business relationship:

- Honeymoon stage: Each party sees the best in the other and the potential of the relationship. Shortcomings, differences and potential issues may be overlooked.
- Power struggle stage: Each party starts to see 'faults' in the other and is sometimes shocked when those issues start to

appear in the relationship. There may be conflict and dissent, with each party needing to be right. Each party is fighting to have his or her voice heard and needs met.
- Dead-zone stage: Both parties tend to withdraw to 'lick their wounds' and think about things. They don't want the relationship to end; but they don't understand the factors at play, so the dynamic becomes 'business as usual', although less productive than it could be. Or the parties realise that there is a problem; but they either don't know what to do about it or are unable to move forward, whether they are aware of the solution or not.
- Partnership stage: The parties resolve their problems and the dynamic becomes one of 'us' rather than 'them and us'. It is productive.
- Leadership stage.

What is interesting about these models is that there are generally teething problems when a new relationship is established. However, most people instinctively shy away from difference, difficulties, disagreement and conflict; so many relationships end up being lost at an early stage. If you can recognise that teething problems are inevitable and are prepared to work through them, you stand a better chance of creating and maintaining more business relationships. This is why conflict management is one of the core relationship management competencies.

Not all relationships are the same. Dwayne D Gremler[140] identified the following types:

- personal – based on the knowledge that each party has of the other;
- formal – based on roles occupied by individuals;
- communal – based on concern for the welfare of others; and
- exchange – based on the giving and receiving of benefits.

How you approach the creation and maintenance of these different types of relationships will depend on their nature and the situation. Naturally, there will be occasions where people have multiple relationships with the same person – for example, when you become friends (social) with your manager (formal), who is also a work colleague (communal). Where there are multiple types of relationships between the same people, difficulties can arise.

(a) Digital relationships

It is increasingly common for business relationships to be initiated and sustained online, through emails, interactions on social media and videoconferencing.

"Early attempts to generate more interactive communications in digital relationships – such as by telephone or face to face – should be made to accelerate, deepen and consolidate these relationships."

How digital relationships are formed and developed can differ from how this generally happens in real life. For example, Tsedal Neeley[141] distinguished between 'swift trust' (where team members learn swiftly to trust one another from the first interaction) and 'passable trust' (linked to online behaviour, where trust is deduced by studying interactions with others).

The coronavirus pandemic has forced us all to grapple with digital relationships, virtual teams and remote collaboration. While the technology is good, it seldom approximates the real-life conditions in which so much important communication – both verbal and non-verbal – takes place. For example, there is a real challenge in creating virtual 'coffee-break moments', where informal social exchanges help to build rapport and trust.

Digital relationships require a host of new protocols and skills, such as:

- screen presence management;
- online authenticity;
- management of non-work related exchanges without breaking confidentiality or privacy rules;
- creation of psychological safety online;
- digital discussion facilitation;

- connection curation;
- micro-move management; and
- online collaboration.

You also need to be particularly aware of distance bias – if you don't see people around you as you would in an office environment, there is a danger that you might accidentally leave them out of discussions and decisions.

Early attempts to generate more interactive communications in digital relationships – such as by telephone or face to face – should be made to accelerate, deepen and consolidate these relationships. At present, however, for social distancing purposes, we must remain in a digital space and build our skill sets accordingly.

John Ingham, author of *The Social Organization,* said recently: "We'll soon need to start thinking less about people as knowledge workers and more about ourselves as relationship workers, where relationships are the core aspect of what we do."[142]

(b) Relationship management skills

Daniel Goleman, an early pioneer of EQ, suggested that the six core skills of relationship management[143] are as follows:

- inspire;
- influence;
- develop;
- initiate change;
- establish team work and collaboration; and
- manage conflict.

Morgan and Hunt[144] explored the variables that impact on commitment and trust in a relationship:

- communication – the openness and honesty of conversations;
- shared values – similarity and alignment in beliefs;
- relationship benefits – what each partner gets out of the relationship;
- acquiescence – the reluctant acceptance of something without protest (suggesting that one party is dominant and the other is sacrificing his or her views or needs);
- propensity to leave – how likely someone is to leave the relationship;
- uncertainty – the level of certainty about each other in the relationship;
- cooperation – how people work together;
- opportunistic behaviour – the extent to which mutual opportunities are seized;

- termination costs – how difficult or costly it is to leave the relationship (some refer to this as 'lock-in' costs); and
- functional conflict – how people resolve differences.

In other models, where there is a focus on emerging client relationships, you might see a relationship model such as the following:

- awareness – where the parties know about each other;
- trust – where trust exists between the parties;
- transaction – where the first piece of business between the two parties takes place;
- satisfaction – where there is satisfaction with what is provided;
- commitment – where there is a level of commitment or loyalty; and
- advocacy – where clients provide positive recommendations and referrals.

A similar approach considers the stages of a client relationship using the metaphor of personal relationships. Many law firms use something similar to classify their most critical client relationships as part of a key account management or account-based marketing programme:

- transactional (dating);
- multi-service (using multiple products and services) (courtship);
- loyal (relationship);
- trusted (engagement);
- partnership (marriage);
- flagship (long marriage); and
- broken (divorce).

Dick and Basu[145] characterised the growth of loyalty through four stages:

- no loyalty;
- spurious loyalty;
- latent loyalty; and
- strong loyalty.

Loyalty can be felt for an individual or for a firm or brand; it is likely that there will be a degree of both.

Many law firms use the Net Promoter Score® (NPS)[146] to assess clients' loyalty and their likelihood of recommending the firm. They ask the question: "On a scale of 1 to 10, where 1 is low and 10 is high, how likely would you be to recommend us?" Those scoring 1 to 6 are seen as detractors; those scoring 7 to 8 are seen as passive supporters; and those scoring 9 and 10 are seen as promoters or advocates.

3.3 Creating rapport and trust

Rapport is a connection. It is built through an unconscious process that takes place alongside communication. Some describe it as a close and harmonious relationship in which people understand each other's feelings and ideas and communicate well. So once again, empathy is critical here.

Some describe rapport as a common perspective, as being 'in sync' or being 'on the same wavelength'. The word 'rapport' comes from the French word meaning to 'bring back' – almost as if we are bringing back the other person's feelings to ourselves.

Some people find it easy to 'click' or connect with other people – they appear to do so naturally. They get to a position of trust and mutual understanding within a few minutes. And while it is true that some personality types find it easier to approach and talk to other people, these skills can be learned and practised by everyone.

Research suggests that most people achieve rapport naturally with between 10% and 30% of people they meet; and with training, most people can double their starting percentage.

"You can build trust and rapport simultaneously. However, rapport focuses more on establishing a bond or connection; whereas trust relies more on building a reputation for reliability and consistency."

(a) Creating rapport

In his book *The Elusive Obvious*, Michael Grinder[147] claimed that there are two broad types of people: dogs and cats. Dogs are the 'pleasers' and are high on rapport. Their voice, pace and energy, hand gestures, head movements, facial expressions and body posture are much more animated than the 'cats', who are independent and high on credibility. I add another type of creature: the bears. These are motivated by power and control.

This dog, cat and bear personality model roughly equates with McLelland's human motivation[148] model – cats are motivated by achievement, dogs by affiliation and bears by power and control. When dogs meet cats, they need to tone down their enthusiastic social banter and focus on the point of the interaction. When a cat meets a dog, both need to turn up their social warmth. Simple adaptations to behaviour – while remaining authentic – enable the interaction to proceed and rapport to form.

According to researchers Linda Tickle-Degnen and Robert Rosenthal,[149] when you have rapport with someone, you share the following qualities:

- Mutual attentiveness: You're both interested in what the other person is feeling, saying or doing.
- Positivity: You're both friendly and upbeat, and show care and concern for each another.
- Coordination: You are 'in sync' with one another, share a common understanding and have similar energy levels, tone of voice and body language.

When you have built rapport with someone, you are better placed to influence, learn from and teach him or her. Rapport is similar to trust. You can build trust and rapport simultaneously. However, rapport focuses more on establishing a bond or connection; whereas trust relies more on building a reputation for reliability and consistency.

The following are all methods that may help in building rapport.

Align your appearance: First impressions count and your appearance should help you to connect with people, not create a barrier. Some psychologists suggest that you should dress just a little 'better' than the people you are about to meet.[150] Others suggest that you should aim to be as similar to them as possible. 'In-group bias' suggests that people feel more comfortable with those whom they consider are similar to them and belong in their group.

Balance communication: Be culturally appropriate with your greeting.

Ask people's names; introduce yourself clearly and confidently. Ask questions to show interest and listen to responses attentively. Keep the information exchange equal.

Find common ground: In Western cultures, most conversations start with 'small talk' about non-contentious issues, such as the weather. This is where you start to explore whether there is some common ground or interest. Most people like talking about themselves and if you show genuine interest by asking questions, they are more likely to relax and open up.

Create shared experiences: Rapport can't grow without interaction and a great way to interact is to create new shared experiences. Shared experiences can be as simple as attending the same conference session together and exchanging views on the venue.

Use empathy: Try to understand how the other person is feeling and thinking – put yourself in his or her shoes and see things from his or her perspective. Ask questions to develop empathy.

Mirror and match behaviour: Research shows that we prefer people who we perceive to be just like ourselves. We subconsciously adapt our style of speaking and behaving when we meet people. Mirroring and matching posture and behaviour are techniques for building rapport by having similar NVC.

If someone's NVC mirrors your own, it is an indication that he or she feels a degree of rapport with you. You can test other people's feelings by changing your stance or position and see whether they follow suit (unconsciously).

(b) How to be liked

While it isn't necessary to be liked in business relationships, it certainly helps when you try to build that initial connection.

Often in business, the common ground is the fact that you work in the same organisation or industry. Or maybe you share social or educational backgrounds or sports interests, or are of a similar age or nationality. You might have acquaintances, friends or associates in common, or a similar view of a topical issue.

How do you encourage people to like you? How do you increase your likeability? Some people call this being personable. Naturally, you want to be authentic – to be the real you.

People will like you if you show an interest in them – by asking questions and taking the time to get to know them. You should share an equal amount of information about yourself. You will need to reveal some of yourself if you want others to open up to you. But in some cultures, it is not socially acceptable to ask people about their personal lives too early in the relationship.

In *How to Win Friends and Influence People*,[151] Dale Carnegie famously said: "You can win more business in two months by being interested in other people than in two years trying to be interesting." Something else that helps with being liked is either to ask for or to give help. Heidi Grant has written an excellent book on asking for help effectively (see p 177).

Keep things positive. No one wants to spend time around a negative or overly critical person. Keep initial conversations upbeat and light – look for the positives. Smile and laugh – others usually join in and it creates a bond. Emotional contagion is powerful.

(c) Creating trust

Trust is a firm belief in the reliability, truth or ability of someone or something. High-competence, low-warmth professionals are often respected, but not trusted.

Diago Gambetta[152] said: "Trust is a means of reducing uncertainty in order that effective relationships can develop." Cousins and Stanwix[153] suggested that trust refers to ideas concerning risk, power and dependency.

Paul A Pavlou[154] argued that there are three outcomes from trust: satisfaction, perceived risk and continuity. Morrison and Firmstone[155] contended that there are several elements to trust: reputation, familiarity/closeness, performance and accountability. Young and Wilkinson[156] claimed that trust is influenced by the duration of the relationship, relative power, the presence of cooperation and environmental factors.

Between businesses, trust might be based on reputation (knowledge of past actions) and brand (a future promise). These ideas are supported by another model of trust. There is inter-firm trust – for example, we may trust brands and organisations that we have heard about.

Then there is inter-personal trust, which is reliant on an individual. This is broken down into two parts. Sensible, rational trust is based on the knowledge and expertise that you demonstrate ('knowing your stuff'), and doing what you say you will do when you say you will do it (reliability). But there is also sensitive or emotional trust, which is based on empathy and EQ.

"Identification-based trust occurs when both parties have a deeper understanding of each other from repeated interactions and each can identify with the goals and objectives of the other. This is a more emotionally driven bond which is harder to break and is the foundation of loyalty."

Management consultants David Maister and Charles H Green have done some interesting research on trust.[157] Their formula is as follows, where T stands for trustworthiness, C for credibility, R for reliability, I for intimacy and S for self-orientation:

$$T = \frac{C + R + I}{S}$$

The key to trust – according to this model – is to minimise your self-interest and concentrate on being credible and reliable, and learning about the other person. Integrity – being honest and having strong moral principles – is also important for establishing trust.

In the digital space, Tsedal Neeley[158] has talked about 'swift trust' (where team members learn to swiftly trust one another from the first interaction) and 'passable trust' (linked to online behaviour, where trust is deduced by studying interactions with others).

In relation to client service, Roy J Lewicki[159] distinguished between different types of trust. Calculus-based trust occurs in the early stages of a relationship, when one party calculates how the other is likely to behave in a given situation and extends trust only insofar as is necessary to achieve a positive outcome. By contrast, identification-based trust occurs when both parties have a deeper understanding of each other from repeated interactions and each can identify with the goals and objectives of the other. This is a more emotionally driven bond which is harder to break and is the foundation of loyalty.

Trust is likewise contextual and varies depending on the situation and circumstances. Engel[160] and others have found that people are more trustworthy if they:

- are elderly;
- are female;
- are communicating face to face; or
- believe that you are deserving.

They found that people are less trustworthy if they:

- can conceal their dishonesty;
- have had to work hard to achieve something to be shared;
- are the kinds of people who talk tough;
- make decisions in a group; or
- are asked repeatedly to be benevolent.

Stephen Covey wrote about the 13 behaviours of high-trust leaders worldwide.[161] Drawing on this and other views, high-trust behaviour appears to have several components:

- shared goals;
- affinity (likeability, attractiveness, empathy and high social sensitivity);
- goodwill (good faith, kindness, sincerity and no hidden agendas);
- fairness and feedback (equality in engagement, explanation and expectation, and psychological safety);
- competence and a perception of errors as learning opportunities;
- communication – especially the ability to say no and share humour; and
- integrity.

One study[162] suggests that two aspects of high-trust teams are critical: equality in engagement in the distribution of conversational turn-taking and high 'average social sensitivity'. Both of these are reliant on good soft skills – the latter on emotional intelligence.

(d) Cross-cultural competency

There are numerous models to help us understand how to adapt our behaviour to make communication and relationships with people from other cultures easier.

The best-known study was by Hofstede,[163] who initially suggested four spectra for cultural behaviour:

- individualistic versus collective;
- masculine versus feminine;
- low power distance versus high power distance; and
- weak uncertainty avoidance versus strong uncertainty avoidance.

He also added a time horizon – short and long-term perspectives. He argued that American and British cultures are highly individualistic and masculine, with low power distance and strong uncertainty avoidance. They are almost polar opposites of many Asian cultures, which are more collective and feminine, with high power distance and weak uncertainty avoidance.

Trompenaars and Hampden-Turner[164] proposed a more detailed version of this model. And in 2005, the Research Project on Leadership Worldwide proposed nine global cultural competencies: universalism and particularism, individualism and communitarianism, specific and diffuse, neutral and affective, achievement and ascription, past and future and internal and external.

P Christopher Earley and Soon Ang[165] also coined the term 'cultural intelligence' (CQ), defined as a person's capability to adapt as he or she

"American and British cultures are highly individualistic and masculine, with low power distance and strong uncertainty avoidance. They are almost polar opposites of many Asian cultures."

interacts with those from other cultures. This is in some ways an extension of EQ. They suggested there are four components to this:

- motivation (CQ drive);
- cognition (CQ knowledge);
- meta-cognition (CQ strategy); and
- behaviour (CQ action).

Cross-cultural, diversity and boardroom skills for barristers

Holly Gavaghan is the business development director at Keating Chambers, which is a leading construction, infrastructure and energy set with 62 members, of whom 28 are queen's counsel (QC). She originally trained as a solicitor at Eversheds and worked in-house at Carillion before working at 39 Essex Chambers, Freshfields and Landmark Chambers.

> *The QC application assessment competencies now include written and oral advocacy, working with others, diversity and integrity. Yet in the past, this was sometimes the first time that barristers – after 20 years of practice – were required to demonstrate their skills beyond technical legal excellence.*

The Bar recently changed the CPD requirements. These now encourage barristers to think about the gaps and establish their own training priorities including, for example, in softer skills such as people management and networking, rather than solely focusing on technical skills.

Barristers must comply with the Bar Standards Board Handbook and Code of Conduct. In October 2015 The Professional Statement was introduced, describing the knowledge, skills and attributes that all barristers should have on 'day one' of practice [www.barstandardsboard.org.uk/uploads/assets/a4556161-bd81-448d-874d40f3baaf8fe2/bsbprofessionalstatementandcompetences2016.pdf]. These include:

- *barristers' distinctive characteristics (legal knowledge, practical knowledge, advocacy and professional standards);*
- *personal values and standards;*
- *working with others; and*
- *management of practice.*

Included in these headings are competencies such as:

- *being aware and active in the pursuit of equality and respect for diversity;*
- *ensuring that they practise with adaptability and flexibility;*
- *being self-aware and self-directed;*
- *recognising and acting upon the continual need to maintain and develop their knowledge and skills;*
- *applying principles of team working; and*
- *understanding the relevance of strategic planning, financial planning and business development in the context in which they work.*

The Professional Statement recognises that it's vital that barristers forge productive relationships internally with their clerks and colleagues and externally with their solicitor and lay clients; and even more so with direct and professional access work.

It's important to balance the barrister skillset of absorbing and presenting often large amounts of information in an articulate way in an adversarial process with the softer skillset of developing excellent relationships. Not always an easy balancing act!

Negotiating settlement of a dispute, for example, needs more than superb advocacy skills. The world has changed and the communication skill set for barristers now requires a more strategic, commercial and empathic approach – more of the softer skills.

A client commented recently that one of our QCs was excellent at persuading board members to settle when they had previously been intent on litigation. That takes gravitas and strategic experience, as well as first-class influencing and persuasion skills. Managing difficult conversations with clients takes highly developed communication, empathy and diplomacy skills, which our barristers and staff demonstrate.

Keating's experience of working closely in teams with solicitor and lay clients at all levels in the construction industry has given our barristers the soft skills needed to communicate effectively with lay clients, witnesses and experts.

Working with diversity is fundamentally important too. We are proud that two of our female QCs were appointed to the Technology and Construction Court in 2016. Four of the nine judges in that court in London are currently female.

Cross-cultural sensitivity

A significant proportion of Keating Chambers' work is outside the United Kingdom. We work on major projects and for clients throughout the Middle East, Hong Kong, South Korea, Australia, Singapore and Africa. Many of these projects involve our clients working in multinational joint ventures. These large, complex cases often involve a team including a QC, numerous juniors, solicitors, experts, local counsel and numerous client representatives in multiple jurisdictions.

One of Keating's strengths is the ability of its barristers to be adaptable and flexible. They develop an understanding of working in dispute resolution in different cultures 'on the job', usually through working in a team with more senior barristers. The same applies to overseas business development trips carried out by barristers and staff.

The applicable governing laws are important; but so too is understanding how to best represent, for example, a client at an arbitration being held in Singapore for South Korean clients in front of a tribunal made up of lawyers from three different legal jurisdictions.

3.4 Navigating difference and conflict

Difference and conflict are inevitable parts of human interaction. Every relationship will experience some element of conflict. Estimates suggest that up to 25% of a manager's time is spent dealing with conflict.

(a) What is conflict?

'Conflict' is "an expressed struggle between at least two independent parties who perceive incompatible goals, scarce resources and interference from others in achieving their goals".[166]

There are generally thought to be five elements to conflict:

- interdependence;
- difference;
- opposition;
- expression; and
- emotion.

An adversarial system has traditionally dominated patterns of human behaviour since the time of the Greek philosophers. However, in the 20th century psychologists Kurt Lewin and Morton Deutsch[167] developed a theory of human behaviour and motivation in groups called 'field theory', and went on to outline the four possible outcomes from conflict using combinations of win and lose. The idea of the 'win-win' also gained currency.

Take different perspectives: In conflict situations, the parties usually have different perceptions about what is happening and punctuate them differently, seeing different start (cause) and end (effect) points.

To enhance empathy skills, Wilmot and Hocker suggest a tool called the 'lens model' of conflict interaction.[168] This involves looking at the conflict as if through a lens – from different angles, zooming in on different aspects and from the other person's perspective.

The key here is to apply person-centred communication, instead of position-centred communication (taking a stand and defending it) or rule-centred communication (asserting the facts).

Identify goals: The key to conflict resolution is to be clear about both your own goals and those of the other party. This can be difficult, as goals can be complex, contradictory and changing.

Manage emotions: Most conflict situations involve emotion, so understanding how to manage both your own emotions and those of others – part of EQ – is critical.

Use power (carefully): John French and Bertram Raven[169] identified five bases of power (or power currencies):

- reward power – the ability to reward;
- coercive power – the ability to punish;
- legitimate power – explicit given cultural roles;
- referent power – from people we are associated with; and
- expert power – based on expertise or knowledge.

Conflict resolution is most effective when there is an equal distribution of power.

Know your conflict style: Kenneth Thomas and Ralph Kilmann[170] identified five conflict strategies and arranged them in a model according to the degree of 'concern for self' and 'concern for the other person' involved in each:

- avoidance – acting as if the conflict does not exist (lose-lose);
- competition – one party tries to get what he or she wants at the other's expense (win-lose);
- compromise – both parties give something up (no win-no lose);
- accommodation – one party gives something up, but doesn't gain (lose-win); and
- collaboration – working together (win-win)

Be principled: Roger Fisher and William Ury,[171] two researchers on the Harvard Negotiation Project, developed four principles for win-win negotiations:

- Separate people from the problem – focus on events and behaviours.
- Focus on interests, not positions – interests are the reasons for the position.
- Generate options for mutual gain – brainstorm multiple options.
- Base choice on objective criteria – find measureable ways to assess the value of suggestions.

They also developed the idea of 'BATNA': the Best Alternative To a Negotiated Arrangement. In negotiation theory, the 'best no-deal option' refers to the most advantageous alternative course of action that can be taken if negotiations fail and an agreement cannot be reached.

Use a framework for negotiation: There are numerous negotiation frameworks to choose from, depending on your preference, the nature and complexity of the problem, and the other party. I use a seven-step process to apply Fisher and Ury's four principles of negotiation:

- Define the conflict issues.
- Identify and evaluate your goals.
- Decide whether you want to negotiate.
- Arrange a meeting.
- Conduct the meeting.
- Make a contract.
- Follow through.

In the Strategic Negotiation course at Harvard Law School,[172] the following seven steps are used:

- Know the key players.
- Know what the key players want.
- "Grow the pie."
- Know when to walk away.
- Define the zone of possible agreement.
- Always aim for a win-win outcome.
- Make concessions.

Listen carefully: Deploy active listening skills to pay attention when the other party speaks. This way, you not only show respect for the other party, but might also learn something that alters the nature of the conflict or points to alternative solutions.

Manage the aftermath: The aftermath of conflict may leave emotional residues, damaged trust and psychological distance. Sometimes differences that cannot be bridged lead to resentment and new conflicts. So action is needed to return to a healthy relationship through acceptance, apology, amends, forgiveness, reconciliation and healing.

Managing conflict and negotiation

Neil Denny has been a family solicitor for 20 years and trained as a qualified mediator. He has worked for Family Law in Partnership and Drewitt Mogers and is currently developing the family department at Roythornes in Nottingham. He has written three books on conflict and collaboration, including *Conversational Riffs: Creating Meaning out of Conflict*.[173]

> *One problem is that solicitor training and the role are rather didactic and focused on telling rather than listening – lawyers are paid to provide advice. Clients want a solution to a problem; yet a lawyer's concern may fall into the need to prove they are right. Lawyers can feel anxious in conflict at the perceived risk to their reputation should they be wrong. At these times, we can double down on proving ourselves right and lose sight of the client's priority in finding a solution.*

When I did my LPC, there was only a half-day session on negotiation skills. Most people assume that solicitors are trained at managing conflict and negotiation, but this is a fallacy. I used to do a beginner's and an intermediate negotiation course for a commercial provider and found that most solicitors – even senior practitioners – lacked even a basic knowledge of the alternative methods of dispute resolution and the negotiation process. These skills should be developed from the very beginning of a solicitor's career.

Lawyers need to be comfortable with conflict and stop seeing it as a threat. We have to acknowledge that conflict in our work is inevitable and stop avoiding it.

Conflict is often pure subjective emotion. As a profession, we think we work with objectivity. That emotion needs to be recognised, reflected and validated; sometimes an apology is all that is needed. In Conversational Riffs, *I advise that people need to recognise when they feel under attack, make a decision not to be defensive with a denial or an excuse, and instead select a different response. Examples might be explicitly acknowledging the other person's position (without conceding they are right) or asking for more information. When we are able to trust these kinds of processes, we become almost like observers and can see how the dynamics within that conflict-charged conversation can change.*

Lawyers can learn to be curious about what might be causing the conflict, and see it as an opportunity to understand the reasons and explore alternative ways to resolve it. All adults need to acknowledge when conflict exists and be willing to step in and navigate the conflict space.

There are so many models. For example, one approach is to avoid opposition and join with the other person in identifying what the problem is – give it a label – and then work together to ask "What can we do to resolve this problem?"

It would be good for the LPC to devote more time to the topic. But as a profession, we need to look at the broader market. There is an immense amount of material around on negotiation and conflict skills. Lawyers need to get curious and pick up one of the many books on the subject, so they can learn about negotiation processes, techniques and tactics. Individuals should develop a self-motivated, self-learning mind-set and be constantly looking at how their skills and performance can be improved. Don't wait to be spoon-fed in short courses. Go and seek this material out for yourself. I always taught newly qualified solicitors to read the reading list: that's why it's there.

I'm often asked if young solicitors can learn from their more experienced colleagues. There is, of course, a great deal that they can learn from senior lawyers; but the risk is that inadequate conflict responses and unwitting, sub-optimal negotiation skills are just perpetuated if those are the behaviours that are being modelled.

4. Leadership – managing a team

Leadership is a major component of soft skills training and essential for all law firms. Most law firms will have some form of leadership development programme. Leadership is a huge topic and one that demands significantly more attention than space allows in this report, so I will concentrate on a few key ideas.

The Center for Creative Leadership suggests there are four fundamental leadership skills:

- self-awareness;
- communication;
- influence; and
- learning agility.[174]

The authors of the *Professional Services Leadership Handbook*[175] offer a leadership model with the following elements:

- self;
- clients;
- people; and
- business.

Apart from sole practitioners, all solicitors will need to learn how to manage a team. Some teams will be permanent and physically close to those in the same discipline; while others may be temporary (for a pitch or a specific assignment), with lawyers from different disciplines, other firms or even other professions.

Frequently, client staff will be part of the team. Increasingly, teams will be remote and/or virtual. And this trend has been accelerated by the coronavirus pandemic. This leaves us open to distance bias, as we tend to focus on the people we see and interact with regularly. This could lead to less vocal team members being overlooked and then feeling isolated.

A legal team manager will want to ensure that new lawyers are provided with the right support to enable them to learn and to develop. The team leader will need to know the strengths and weaknesses – as well as the aspirations – of each team member, in order to allocate tasks that provide sufficient stretch without causing harmful stress that puts the client's work at risk.

Most lawyers will be highly competent in how to supervise the technical work of team members. This is enshrined in a firm's quality management, risk management and compliance processes. But the softer skills of delegation, coaching and providing feedback are sometimes less developed, with team managers in smaller firms often being left to learn through trial and error.

Being an authentic leader

Oliver Taylor is marketing manager at Mundays in Surrey. His 15-year career has been committed to legal firms.

Lawyers are all cut from the same cloth – academically smart and incredibly focused and dedicated individuals. The next generation have those same extraordinary attributes, but also manage to bring more of their authentic selves to their work life.

It is about being human. Years of studying with certificates proudly framed on the wall doesn't create a rite of passage for an alter ego in the office. Too many times, I have seen two sides of lawyers: in the office, they are no-nonsense powerhouses; and at home, they are devoted, caring family members. Yes, we are working in a professional environment; and yes, hierarchy is important; but being more authentic will make you a better leader and help you get more out of colleagues.

You learn something new every day. Everyone is still a student. No one knows everything. You need to show some vulnerability and allow others to help you. Lawyers need to listen more – to the views and ideas of others – to find the best solutions. Each generation educates the others. 'The Originals' pass down life skills, confidence and advice. 'The Next Generation' can upskill others with their fresh approach to technology.

Trust and respect are critical. Seniority comes with time in the game, but everyone wants to be treated with respect. Trust your colleagues – they have the same interests at heart and will follow the same values to ensure clients receive the best service.

People have different styles and approaches, but this doesn't mean that they are wrong. Lawyers need to appreciate the value of diversity. Trust must be embedded in working relationships – believe that work will be completed and returned when and how it was requested. Respect is earned through valuing and trusting colleagues.

Respect can be lost faster than it is gained. And it's hard to win it back once damaged. Juniors and new starters quickly learn from the grapevine who's who, how they operate and their working standards. This will subconsciously paint you with a brush that is hard to shift – treat everyone fairly and your image won't be murky from the start.

Remember that support teams are there to support the firm. Lawyers are their clients, so don't make unrealistic demands and constantly moan. Some results take time to unfold. Lawyers need to listen to and understand everyone to ensure that a well-balanced, communicative and happy team is built from the outset.

4.1 Delegation

Delegation is a frequent topic of conversation in law firms – whether it's to free up the time of leaders, empower new leaders, develop teams or work more efficiently. Traditional pyramid structures in professional service firms require that a senior person build a team of junior people in order to achieve maximum profitability. Delegation is a vital element of this process.

(a) Supervision versus delegation

Supervision and delegation are not the same thing. Supervision relates to the professional responsibility to manage risk and ensure quality. It helps with the observance of procedure and the sharing of best practice. Professional bodies usually have specific requirements for supervising trainees.

Delegation is the act of empowering another and assigning responsibilities. It is likely that you will want to heavily supervise those to whom you are delegating for the first time. Both have a role to play in training and development.

Typically, though, a directive approach is needed for supervision (of juniors) and a more consultative style for delegation (to seniors).

(b) Supervision and delegation skills

Supervisors need excellent technical knowledge, as this is one of the main things that they are assessing. However, it is possible to delegate tasks – such as management and client relationship tasks – where technical knowledge might not be paramount and other skills are required.

Communication and feedback skills are required for both supervision and delegation. It is important that an appreciative approach (more positive feedback than constructive criticism) is adopted where possible, to strengthen people's confidence.

Coaching skills are important too – asking questions to encourage people to try to find answers and solutions for themselves, rather than simply telling them the answer. This builds knowledge and self-confidence, as well as important skills for problem solving.

(c) When to delegate

Before delegating, you need to analyse and categorise the types of work to be delegated. Some may be repetitive, routine and procedural tasks, for which there are prescribed methods, documented processes and online templates or standards. Some may be unusual or unique problem-solving activities, where a degree of critical thinking is required. Others may require a broader and deeper range of commercial knowledge and skills, and the ability to deal with challenging people.

While people often consider delegating when they are busy and over-stretched, it is important to remember that it takes time to delegate

"While some leaders will delegate happily to their team until someone indicates that he or she has too much work, others will be overprotective and take on more themselves to avoid making their team members work too hard. Obviously, a good leader will achieve a balance once he or she fully understands the capabilities and limits of his or her team members."

tasks properly – to provide clear instructions, to support the person in learning how to tackle a new or complex task, and to check in regularly on progress.

(d) Why don't people delegate more?

The business case for delegation is strong. But many people nonetheless fail or refuse to delegate. There are many reasons for this, which must be investigated and addressed.

Worrying reasons why people don't delegate include a lack of trust in the skills and abilities of those available for delegation; and 'work hugging' – a fear that if work is delegated, personal fee targets won't be achieved and there will then be an onus to generate new work.

While some leaders will delegate happily to their team until someone indicates that he or she has too much work, others will be overprotective and take on more themselves to avoid making their team members work too hard. Obviously, a good leader will achieve a balance once he or she fully understands the capabilities and limits of his or her team members.

(e) Delegation steps

A starting point is to consider the suitability of the individual for the task – his or her skill level, workload and personal style. There are numerous models to support you in tackling all the necessary steps in delegation.

Ros Jay and Richard Templar[176] have suggested that the art of delegation comprises the following steps:

- Review the task and set the objective.
- Decide to whom to delegate.
- Set the following parameters:
  - objective;
  - deadline;
  - quality standards;
  - budget;
  - limits of authority; and
  - details of any resources available.
- Check that the delegatee understands.
- Give the person back-up.

I propose a slightly different approach:

- Clarify expectations:
  - Explain what needs to be accomplished and why it's important.

  - Help the delegatee to see the big picture and context – connect the task to organisational, team, client or personal development goals.
  - Explore the expectations of both parties.
  - Agree the parameters.

- Establish checkpoints:
  - Plan how to ensure that the work is being completed by establishing checkpoints – these might be more regular for a junior who is tackling a task for the first time.
  - Manage the risk of mistakes occurring by being proactive and staying in the loop at critical points.

- Delegate the results, not the process:
  - Focus on the end result and, unless the delegatee is inexperienced or there are prescribed regulations, allow him or her to determine how best to achieve it. If you dictate exactly what to do, when to do it and how to do it, you limit the learning potential.

- Define roles:
  - Explain how much support you will provide, and when and how.
  - Let the delegatee know when to wait for your instructions or make independent recommendations and decisions. The more authority you give him or her, the better the end result will be.
  - Make sure that the delegatee understands the extent to which independent initiative is allowed.
  - Encourage questions and be available to offer help and guidance.
  - Signpost other sources of help and support.
  - Describe the situations in which the delegatee should definitely report back.

- Talk about consequences:
  - Reassure the delegatee about time recording – it may take him or her longer to complete an unfamiliar task. He or she will need to do this even if it isn't reflected in the billing.
  - If you give people greater authority over their work, inform them of the consequences of both successful and unsuccessful results. What rewards can they expect if they do a great job? What will happen if they don't achieve the expected results?

- Confirm understanding:
  - Ask the delegatee to repeat back his or her understanding of

the task – and possibly even to email you the key points and schedule the checkpoints in your calendar.
- Ask him or her what he or she is likely to tackle first (and why), and what he or she perceives to be the most challenging aspects of the task.

(f) Mutual responsibility

Those delegating tasks have a responsibility to provide clear instructions, context, support and help.

Those performing delegated tasks also have responsibilities – they should:

- be honest about their skill levels and their workload if they think that this may impact on their ability to complete the task;
- ask questions to obtain clarification and seek support when needed;
- speak to the delegator if they foresee any difficulties – particularly if they suspect that critical dates or quality levels might not be achieved; and
- ensure that they report back on the agreed check points and do not exceed the limits of their authority.

(g) Delegation best practice

From the numerous training sessions that I have run on delegation, the following points may also prove helpful:

- Empathy: Try to remember when you first tackled a new task and were on the receiving end of delegation. Put yourself in the shoes of the delegatee and try to address likely questions and concerns.
- NVC: Watch the NVC of the delegatee – in particular, to see whether his or her body language changes and if so, at what point. Consider whether he or she is signalling either resistance or the desire to ask a question.
- Personality differences: People come in all shapes and sizes. Some are more focused on the task and others on relationships; some are introverts and others are extroverts. Take particular care when delegating to those who have a different style, as the way they prefer to communicate or work may be different from yours.
- Reassurance: Explain that elements of the task are tricky and that you yourself experienced some difficulty when tackling the task for the first time. Give people permission to express their concerns.
- Reflection: Once you have explained the task, allow the delegatee some time to reflect on what needs to be done and to return for further clarification or help.

"People come in all shapes and sizes. Some are more focused on the task and others on relationships; some are introverts and others are extroverts. Take particular care when delegating to those who have a different style, as the way they prefer to communicate or work may be different from yours."

- Feedback: Once the task is completed, ask the delegatee for feedback on how you might improve the way you delegate tasks in future.

4.2 Coaching

A team leader needs to coach people. Unlike mentoring, where the mentor imparts his or her wisdom and knowledge, coaching is designed to help people think for themselves and find their own ideas and solutions. Coaching is a distinct discipline with its own professional guidelines and qualifications, although all managers can learn the basic principles and apply them in their day-to-day dealings with team members.

Coaching involves many different skills, such as listening, paying attention, offering perspective, exploring for information, solving problems, creating solutions, managing performance, providing feedback, motivating, teaching and guiding.

A simple, well-known coaching framework was developed by John Whitmore.[177] His GROW model (goals; reality; options; will to act) structures a series of questions designed to help people reach their own conclusions about what they want and need to do. The coachee builds self-confidence from deciding what he or she needs to do, rather than being told.

As people are often unclear about their goals when they start coaching, it helps to begin with questions about their current situation or reality. This enables the team leader to obtain background information about the coachee and his or her work, and to start thinking about what sorts of goals the coachee is likely to need. It also helps to establish a relationship of openness, interest and trust.

(a) Reality testing – understanding the current situation

With coaching, questions are used to lead people to explore their values, views, motivations, options and actions in a structured way, and to help them reality-test their goals and plans.

We know from the latest research on insight selling[178] that people are more likely to be persuaded when someone asks insightful questions, provides additional ideas and information with those questions, educates and challenges them, and creates an impact by asking the right questions.

Coaching aims to help people break out of their old ways of thinking and behaving. Human beings are creatures of habit: doing things in the way we have done them in the past is safe and relatively low risk. To try something new is risky – both to our reputation and to our relationships.

"Coaching aims to help people break out of their old ways of thinking and behaving. Human beings are creatures of habit: doing things in the way we have done them in the past is safe and relatively low risk. To try something new is risky – both to our reputation and to our relationships."

By asking questions, we allow people to explore their inner world; and we can also begin to understand their mental model and perspective. People need to reflect on what has happened in the past, what worked and what didn't, and how they would like things to be different in the future.

Questions also encourage the coachee to think about other people's perspectives, which may be different from his or her own. They can help the coachee to develop empathy with colleagues and clients. Just as in selling, we use questions to explore afflictions (from which people want to move away) and aspirations (to which people want to move towards). Questions help us to understand the motivations for a particular individual.

We use questions to build a compelling view of the past and to think about the future. We use questions to help the individual consider the downsides of not acting and the upsides of changing.

(b) Goal setting

Through coaching, we provide a safe environment where people can express their views, questions and even fears in confidence, and explore what they want and need to do in their own way.

The coachee needs to think about his or her goals. These may be short, medium and long term. They may be focused on current work activities or tasks, on the coachee's personal life or on his or her career.

Once the coachee is clear about his or her goals, it becomes easier to identify strategies and options for achieving those goals. Once there is a goal, it is possible to measure progress.

When we tell people to do something, we are likely to meet resistance. And when people are told to do something, they are less likely to be committed to doing it than if they come up with the idea themselves. People need to set their own goals – although they may need help in aligning these goals with those of the organisation or team.

Aims might be general; but goals or objectives are better if they are SMART. Sometimes, goals need to be broken down into bite-sized pieces. A stepping-stone approach may at times be helpful (see p 84).

Dr Gail Matthews, psychology professor at the Dominican University in California,[179] found that written goals are 42% more likely to be achieved.

(c) Option development
People often get stuck because they can only see one route forward, which for some reason is not palatable or feasible.

Coaching questions help the coachee to think through what else he or she might do and consider other options. He or she might be asked about what has worked in the past and what he or she could do differently in the future; about what has worked for others; and about what people he or she admires might do under similar circumstances. The questions may prompt research and analysis.

Questions should seek to explore any limiting assumptions that may be preventing someone from setting or attempting to achieve a goal. If the coachee lacks self-confidence, questions might help him or her to reflect on past successes and strengths to move past those limiting assumptions.

Questions can also help the coachee to consider the pros and cons of different options, and to choose the most appropriate course of action.

(d) Will or commitment to act
We use questions to test what might be involved in a plan and to ensure that people have considered all possible steps that they need to take and barriers to overcome to achieve their goals. We might ask what the coachee needs to do to take the first step; what he or she needs to do to maintain momentum; and what he or she anticipates might get in the way of making progress.

In the final stage of coaching, we must consider whether the coachee is in a place where he or she can make progress towards his or her goals. This might involve asking what can be reasonably achieved in the short term – bite-sized, manageable activities that can be completed before the next coaching session.

(e) Latest developments in the neuroscience of coaching
I was particularly struck by the findings in a 2019 book called *Helping People Change: Coaching with Compassion for Lifelong Learning and Growth*.[180] Using the latest neuroscience findings, the organisational behaviourist authors offer some simple key messages – notably, the power of visualising your ideal self and future vision to generate a PEA (see p 68).

They suggest focusing on strengths rather than correcting weaknesses or ensuring compliance with externally sourced targets which triggers an NEA – a stress response when we consider what we ought or should do. They argue that the desire to change must outweigh the obligation to change.

The authors outline the stages of their intentional change theory (ICT):

- Identify the ideal self and personal vision.
- Explore the real self – both strengths and weaknesses.
- Establish a learning agenda.
- Experiment with and practise new behaviour.
- Maintain resonant relationships (based on mindfulness, a positive emotional tone, the arousal of hope, an authentic connection and compassion) and social identity groups.

For effective coaching, the authors argue that the coach must form a resonant relationship with the coachee. The authors offer the concept of a 'high-quality connection', and suggest that the coach must have 'emotional-carrying capacity', adaptability and connection, as well as shared vision, shared compassion and shared relational energy.

This echoes the ideas of the humanist approach in psychotherapy, where the essential components of the helper include the following:

- empathy – the ability to see the other person's perspective;
- congruence – authenticity and the expression of honest views and reactions; and

"Questions should seek to explore any limiting assumptions that may be preventing someone from setting or attempting to achieve a goal. If the coachee lacks self-confidence, questions might help him or her to reflect on past successes and strengths to move past those limiting assumptions."

- unconditional positive regard – a lack of judgement and a genuinely positive attitude towards the coachee.

Coachees must also have resonant relationships with those around them – their line managers and peers. Any new behaviour must be supportive of their personal identity and reinforced by peers in their social identity groups.

In most business situations, focus is something that is valued. But the authors explore an interesting downside of focus: that we then fail to notice other things around us or other possibilities. They describe the science of two brain networks: the analytic network, used for analysing and completing tasks; and the empathic network, used for relationships. They argue that when focused on a task, we can inadvertently miss what is going on with the people around us. This supports earlier leadership models, which show how leaders must balance their attention on the task at hand with individual and team relationships.

Returning to neuroscience, the authors explain the differences between:

- the autonomic nervous system, which is responsible for regulating the body's unconscious actions;
- the parasympathetic nervous system (PNS), which is responsible for the 'rest-and-digest' and 'feed-and-breed' activities that occur when the body is at rest; and
- the sympathetic nervous system (SNS), which is responsible for the fight-or-flight response.

Their research shows that coaching questions sparking joy, gratitude and curiosity activate the PNS; whereas negative questions trigger the SNS. This is why they suggest focusing on the coachee's personal aims, vision and strengths, rather than weaknesses or failures to achieve previous or external goals that have been set.

The authors also mention the renewal system, in which the PNS battles the SNS –an elaboration of the old left brain-right brain idea. As coaching aims to help people identify and develop more options to achieve their goals, it is important that they are open to creative ideas. It takes a skilled coach to notice when the coachee is in problem-solving mode or is open to new ideas, and when he or she might be moving towards a stress response.

The authors also state: "To make changes stick, our research shows that it has to be intentionally and internally motivated rather than imposed from the outside."[181] They warn that the coaching process is not straightforward. They cite research confirming that behaviour change occurs not in a linear fashion, but rather in discontinuous bursts or spurts, which they describe as 'discoveries'.

Five such discoveries – mapping onto the stages outlined above in the ICT – are required for a sustained change in behaviour. This means that the coach must be compassionate and may have to spend significant time working on each of the steps while the coachee transitions at his or her own speed:

- ideal self and personal vision;
- real self;
- learning agenda;
- experiments and practice; and
- resonant relationships.

Coaching to develop soft skills for legal leaders

Alyson Pellowe is a director of People Vision. She is an experienced HR and learning and development professional who provides executive coaching in the property, healthcare and government sectors.

There's a challenge for professionals, as they are generally so good at their technical day jobs that they find themselves promoted to head of department, where they are faced with a host of team and performance management issues for which they are unprepared.

By the time lawyers get to a senior level, they are less malleable and time poor, and don't want to be trained with other people, but rather coached or mentored on a bespoke, one-to-one basis. This is a safer and more efficient learning environment for them.

Once in a productive coaching relationship – after confidentiality and goals issues have been tackled – they can address the needs of their team as well as their own development needs. There are various tools that can be used to start things off – such as appraisals, psychometric assessments and 360-degree feedback. These can highlight areas to work on.

They will need to know how to develop a high-performance team and to be the very best role models. A frequent challenge is their span of control – it is impossible to manage a team where there are over 20 direct reports, so helping them restructure the team is a topic that frequently arises. Other common issues include using established frameworks for team development – which may not exist in smaller firms – and remote working,

While some organisations will address needs across the practice and provide 'sheep-dip' training or coaching programmes for everyone, each learning situation is different. There can be engagement and motivation issues if the same approach is applied to everyone; and this can be inefficient.

Coaching can also be provided effectively and efficiently through digital channels such as Skype or other videoconferencing platforms. And if the environment is right and diaries can be coordinated, peer group coaching and action learning sets can be effective interventions. These can also help leaders to develop their own coaching skills, which will benefit their teams.

Some people need regular and intensive coaching; others need more sporadic help when they reach key milestones or transitions in their careers, such as becoming qualified, being promoted, leading a team, gaining a new client or new responsibilities, or stepping up to a managing partner role. It can be lonely at the top. There's also an argument for consistent coaching so that people continue to hone their skills throughout their careers.

4.3 Feedback

The art and science of providing feedback effectively often arises in training workshops on change management, team development, performance management, delegation and coaching.

(a) 'Feedback' defined

Kate Ludeman[182] suggests that effective feedback involves paying attention, providing high-quality information, empathising, appreciating and helping the person to switch into a learning mode.

We can minimise stress and conflict by giving feedback on performance in a positive way. It should be seen as a way to increase self-awareness, offer options and encourage learning, rather than being judgemental and critical.

(b) Feedback can hurt

In an article on the art and science of giving and receiving criticism at work, Courtney Seiter said: "We remember criticism strongly but inaccurately if it conflicts with our self-image. Negativity bias means we remember negative things more strongly."[183]

We should remember that we all differ when it comes to what feedback we want and how we react to feedback.

Research by Naomi Eisenberger[184] has shown that the brain treats social pain in much the same way as physical pain. Giving positive feedback can activate the brain's reward centres in a similar way to financial windfalls. Five social rewards are deeply important to the brain: status, certainty, autonomy, relatedness and fairness. People can experience feedback as an attack on their 'status', which to the brain is perceived in a similar way to a physical attack.

(c) Feedback for motivation

Feedback is important for motivation. The Progress Principle study[185] found that there are three types of feedback:

- nourishing events that are uplifting (eg, praise or emotional support);
- catalytic events that help work tasks (eg, the provision of training or resources); and
- progress events (eg, receiving feedback on progress in meaningful work).

The study found that employees' 'best' days involved progress events.

(d) Offer a 'feedback sandwich'

Many people are familiar with the idea of a 'feedback sandwich', in which the more critical material is wrapped up in positive layers. Start with a positive comment and appreciation for effort or work done well;

"We can minimise stress and conflict by giving feedback on performance in a positive way. It should be seen as a way to increase self-awareness, offer options and encourage learning, rather than being judgemental and critical."

> *"When providing feedback, comment only on behaviour (which can be changed), and never on the person or personality (which cannot be changed). Use empathy to try to understand the person's perspective by asking questions and creating joint ownership."*

then mention the areas requiring change and improvement, before ending with more positive comments. Keep language descriptive rather than evaluative.

Ask for explanations and offer alternatives. Always leave people with a choice. Be careful on the timing of feedback: provide it as soon as possible, but pick your moment. Ideally, feedback should be given on a regular basis. *The One Minute Manager*[186] has some good suggestions on 'instant praisings' and 'catching people doing things right'.

(e) Create an appreciative environment

In her book *Time to Think*,[187] psychologist Nancy Kline discussed research indicating that a 5:1 ratio of appreciation to criticism creates a psychologically safe environment (appreciative environment). This enables people to feel safe speaking up, asking questions and contributing. It therefore builds people's confidence and helps them to think for themselves.

She argued that change is best facilitated in the context of genuine praise. She said that society teaches us that to be positive is to be naïve and vulnerable; whereas to be critical is seen as informed, buttressed and sophisticated. The evidence suggests that a more positive atmosphere has many benefits for wellbeing and productivity.

(f) Emotional contagion

We need to be aware of the impact of our own emotions on those around us. 'Emotional contagion' is a neurobiological term that describes how your behaviour can lift or deflate the team. A shared mood unites a team. Teams with a positive joint experience perform better. Positive behaviours (eg, empathy and mirroring) create a connection between a leader's brain and the brains of others.

(g) How to provide feedback

When providing feedback, comment only on behaviour (which can be changed), and never on the person or personality (which cannot be changed). Use empathy to try to understand the person's perspective by asking questions and creating joint ownership. Consider positives as well as negatives. Make it constructive: how could things be done better? Build confidence; don't destroy it. Make practical suggestions. Agree action points for the future (and follow up). Extract learning points for everyone.

The content of your feedback should be information specific (ie, provide examples), issue focused and based on observation. Your manner will be important too – you need to be direct and sincere, and 'own' the feedback.

Geoffrey James[188] offers 10 rules for giving feedback:

- Avoid providing negative feedback and criticism.
- Don't hoard or store up negative or critical feedback.
- Never use feedback to express your anger or frustration.
- Don't use email to convey negative feedback.
- Start with real and sincere compliments.
- Explore the cause of the problem.
- Listen first.
- Ask questions that encourage and develop self-awareness.
- Support the development of the behaviours you want to see.
- Ask for feedback and be prepared to listen and accept it.

(h) Reacting to feedback

> *Feedback is a gift. Ideas are the currency of our next success. Let people see you value both feedback and ideas.*
> Jim Trinka and Les Wallace[189]

When feedback is rejected, it is often because it has set off a truth, relationship or identity trigger.

Here are some rules for receiving feedback:

- Avoid defensiveness.
- Show vulnerability.
- Ask for specific examples.
- Ask for clarification.
- Provide another perspective.
- Separate the accurate from the inaccurate information.
- Ask what you can do to improve in future.
- Agree goals and a follow-up.

(i) Feedback and millennials (generational differences)
A 2014 *Harvard Business Review* article by Jack Zenger and Joseph Folkman, entitled "Your employees want the negative feedback you hate to give",[190] reported on the results of research into 899 individuals, 49% of whom were based in the United States.

The research showed that people value corrective feedback even more than praise if it is provided constructively. By roughly a 3:1 margin, people believe it does more to improve their performance than positive feedback.

Generally speaking, the older the research participants were, the more feedback they wanted of both kinds. The Boomers showed a much stronger preference for both giving positive feedback and receiving negative feedback than the other two groups; while the young Gen Y-ers did not seem to feel comfortable giving even positive feedback.

(j) Understand the change cycle
Change is rarely immediate; instead, there is a change cycle. The original model of the change cycle was developed by Elisabeth Kübler-Ross[191] and indicates that energy levels fluctuate as people move through the following stages:

- shock;
- denial;
- anger;
- depression;
- acceptance (bargaining);
- experimentation; and
- success.

Lewin's model of change[192] suggested that first you need to help people 'unfreeze' by reducing the threat and creating psychological safety before changing the behaviour and 're-freezing'.

5. Business development – marketing, selling and referrer management
The subject that generated most debate and feedback in the research

for this report was business development and client relationship management. The persistence of the rainmaker concept (and the 'finders, minders and grinders' phrase) is perhaps explained by the fact that those valuable skills are so rare in the legal profession.

At the core of this issue are the differences between the outlooks and skills needed to be a technical expert and those needed to be a good relationship manager, as outlined in Table 7.

Table 7. Outlooks and skills of technical specialists versus relationship managers

Technical specialist	Relationship manager
Case or transaction focus	Relationship focus
Fees for self or team	Fees for firm
Narrow focus	Broad focus
Contact as needed	Regular contact
Few, specialist contacts	Many commercial contacts
Mostly speak and advise	Mostly ask and listen
Short term and immediate	Long term and future
Technical skills	Commercial skills
Specialist	Generalist

While most lawyers will have access to teams of internal and external marketing and business development professionals, few have a deep understanding of what these functions are trained to do.

There are several levels of professional qualification (ie, foundation certificate, certificate, diploma, postgraduate diploma and apprenticeships) for marketers in the United Kingdom, provided by the Chartered Institute of Marketing (CIM); although many people in business development roles do not possess professional qualifications. Increasingly, experienced lawyers are assuming roles in business development.

5.1 What is business development?

I have found that it helps to talk about business development for lawyers by considering three distinct processes:

- marketing (ie, research and analysis, planning, segmentation, positioning, value proposition development, content development, profile raising and lead generation);

- selling (ie, lead nurturing, relationship development, pitching, conversion); and
- relationship management (ie, client experience management, service delivery, client development, cross-selling, account management, collaboration, referral management).

Some of these are more relevant for established lawyers than new lawyers; some are more relevant for those marketing to businesses and intermediaries (as opposed to private individuals); and some are more relevant for those marketing particular legal services – such as dispute resolution or employment law. Collectively, I call this skill set 'clientology'.

Much marketing theory initially focused on how to promote products to consumers (ie, business-to-consumer marketing). Techniques were then developed to market products to businesses (ie, business-to-business (B2B) marketing). Then services marketing emerged, within which the marketing of professional services is a distinct discipline.

How legal services are marketed is fundamentally different from how other services are marketed. And the approach when marketing legal services to other organisations can be quite different from that when marketing legal services to individuals or private clients.

In March 2020 LexisNexis InterAction[193] reported that that only 49% of US firms identified their business development efforts as successful, and just 25% of firms in Europe and Asia Pacific. Cross-firm collaboration remains a challenge.

Embracing technology to develop relationship management skills

Fiona Jackson is client adviser at LexisNexis InterAction – one of the most popular CRM systems in law firms globally.

Gone are the days when a move in-house for lawyers was considered a professional compromise. Today, fewer senior associates are choosing the path to law firm partnership – either due to limited opportunities as a result of new law firm business models or by choice. Lawyers are attracted by the salaries, work-life balance and kudos that they get from being general counsel (GC).

The role of the GC is evolving too. With the provision of legal advice as a given, the GC is expected to take on the mantle of a strategic adviser, identifying new opportunities for business growth, mergers and acquisitions, forays into other regions and so on.

Consequently, their demands on law firms are changing. Fee earners in law firms are expected to help the GC fulfil the role of a strategic business driver. Law firms need to assist by proactively spotting emerging business trends and opportunities, which the GC can take to the board. This inculcates trust in the law firm and so strengthens the GC-law firm relationship.

Gaining the trust of the GC for commercial benefit requires a concerted business development effort by the law firm. Core to this effort is an in-depth understanding of the GC's organisation, market sector and personal challenges – all of which combined delivers 'the' client experience to the legal department. This is potentially where fee-earners find themselves at a crossroads – as legal practitioners, they want to practise law, not get involved in business development or relationship building. If 'client experience' is where the battle is fought and won, how can firms differentiate themselves? The answer is a resounding "Through the strength of their relationships."

"That's easily said!" is often the response from lawyers. Naturally, cultivating and building relationships is an art form that requires a certain personality (gregarious and outgoing), which not all lawyers have. To all the naysayers and reluctant relationship managers: technology can help fee earners and law firms to shine by embedding measurable business development in their day-to-day activities and making relationship management intuitive.

The reality, of course, is that while junior lawyers and millennials are cleverly embracing technology, the more senior fee earners and partners need 'technology done to' them. So be it; but rest assured – it'll still work! A Magic Circle law firm is successfully leveraging its CRM technology to strengthen its position in the banking sector. For 20 key clients and prospects, the firm has established a business development and relationship building programme to achieve its goal. The CRM system is enabling the firm to tangibly monitor and measure progress of the business development effort, engagement and the corresponding gains being made in relationship strength.

A key component of superior client experience is a firm's ability to provide holistic, bespoke, cross-practice and personal advice. CRM technology enables this by facilitating a complete picture of the client and the involvement of the firm's stakeholders by leveraging data from multiple sources and across the personal, professional and organisational spheres.

Technology helps to mitigate relationship risk too, which is of vital importance in a people-driven business. Firms can ensure that relationships are spread across multiple people, so that in the event of one individual leaving, the business isn't at risk. A classic example is in the context of 'succession planning'. Often, firms know well in advance that a partner is retiring, but only realise post-departure that the individual was the only person with a relationship with a key high-billing client. With a CRM system, this gap in relationship would be highlighted from the get-go.

With client experience being the number one differentiator, proactive and measurable technology-supported relationship management is a powerful capability to have.

Many soft skills are involved in marketing, selling and relationship management. I have selected three specific skills that arise regularly in the course of my work with clients and that were mentioned during the interviews for this report.

5.2 Networking

Many law firms use networking as part of their marketing, sales and relationship management strategies. For young lawyers, this starts with a focus on raising their profile and establishing relationships internally.

More experienced lawyers see networking as a way to maintain contact with existing clients and referrers, and also to meet new contacts. As face-to-face contact remains so important in establishing rapport and trust, the traditional methods of networking – at your own seminars, at third-party conferences and at business, technical and professional association meetings – are preferred. But globalisation and the digital revolution – not to mention the recent public health constraints due to the coronavirus pandemic – have increased the prevalence of online networking.

Networking requires the use of numerous personal and interpersonal skills, as well as a framework for their effective application in particular situations. Networking effectiveness is increased when lawyers have realistic expectations and some selling expertise or experience.

Networking, selling and referrer management skills

Helen Peach, a barrister and solicitor working primarily in dispute resolution and mediation, has practised law for over 25 years at firms including Buss Murton, Armsworth Alexander and Rix & Kay. Before that, she held senior sales management roles in the executive recruitment market.

Lawyers are particularly bad at soft skills and recognising how they need them as businesspeople.

While lawyers may acknowledge the need for management skills, sometimes older lawyers see 'selling' as a dirty word. It scares them. But every professional has to learn how to identify opportunities, ask for work and close the deal. Lawyers can also be rather shy about promoting themselves. Training in this area should be part of the LPC – every lawyer needs to know how to promote their business. We need to recognise that as a profession, we lag way behind accountants in this regard.

A key method of promotion is networking and Tunbridge Wells is a good area with lots of opportunities to do so. But you have to prepare yourself for networking and think about what you might say, what you might learn and how you might use it. I just received a really nice piece of litigation business as a result of directing work I don't do on evicting tenants to another lawyer. Referrer management is often overlooked. It's unrealistic to expect one networking event to generate work – you have to learn to connect other people, provide opportunities for others and stay in touch, so that when a need arises, they think of you.

It can take 30 hours to put a seminar talk together for just 16 clients who already know you – so you have to work hard at using the content in social media and inviting referrers and their clients along, and be clever about using that content in other ways.

I believe these skills can be taught to lawyers – either internally or by outside experts. But trainers need to understand the nature of the legal services market; otherwise, the sales techniques provided don't fit. There's lots of training out there which equates selling law with selling widgets.

My training as a barrister provided many skills that can be used in presentations – projecting your voice, speaking with confidence and anticipating questions.

Lawyers are trained to record whatever we do, so there is a tendency to use emails and written communication. But it is so much better for developing relationships if we use the phone, where you can pick up nuances and explore personal and social issues. That's a skill that requires training, so that you develop confidence in conversations. I have noticed that the junior members of the profession are particularly loath to pick up the phone; and I spend a lot of time explaining how easy it is to delete an email unread, whereas most people are too polite to just put the phone down!

As well as training, internal communications can help a lot with business development. Lawyers need signposting information to know what their colleagues can do and, for example, what languages they speak if they are to be effective at cross-selling. Those are internal networking skills. There is also a mind-set that should see everyone as having valuable contacts – whether it is a secretary or one of the senior support people.

When it comes to networking skills, I usually break the process down into stages.

(a) Advance planning

Lawyers need to analyse their existing clients, referrers and sources of work, and establish goals for what they want to achieve through networking. They need to identify the best places to network, where they are most likely to meet the types of people they are targeting. Ideally, they need to have a plan – for themselves, their team, their territory or their firm.

Then they need to undertake some preparation, which might include the following steps:

- Manage expectations: Networking is a valuable source of market intelligence. You can see it as a learning experience; as a way to keep your firm's name on people's radar; and, of course, as a way to initiate new conversations.
- Research the trends and issues affecting those who will be at the networking event: This allows you to focus conversations on areas of shared interest.
- Research the nature and roles and organisations of the people you are likely to meet: This allows you to quickly identify those where there are existing relationships or where a relationship could be particularly beneficial.
- Ensure clarity of messaging: Consider how you will introduce yourself, what you want people to remember about you and the particular messages or services you hope to convey. Lawyers need to know how best to introduce themselves and be armed with some stories relating to the services they are promoting. Management professor Keith Rollag[194] has said: "Surprisingly large numbers of professionals do less than their best because they haven't mastered three basic yet critical getting to know you skills: introducing themselves, remembering people's names and asking questions."

(b) Performance at the event

- Attendance: Some lawyers like to arrive early; others prefer to arrive later when people are already assembled. I encourage lawyers to 'hunt in a pack' and attend events with a colleague who has a slightly different personality, to remove the challenge of approaching people alone.
- NVC: Lawyers need to adopt a positive mind-set so that this is communicated through their NVC. They should also be adept at reading the NVC of others, to see where they might join a group, when to ask questions and how to manage the interaction.
- Approaches and introductions: Lawyers need to develop strategies to approach people, introduce themselves and join conversations. They need to know how to structure initial introductions so that a conversation flows naturally.
- Questions and listening: You need to ask questions to develop your empathy with people, to show interest and to identify areas of common interest. Lawyers should listen actively to what is being said, so that they can explore more deeply and provide relevant information in response.
- Identify reasons to follow up: If you meet someone that you would like to talk to further, you need to identify a reason to exchange contact details and agree, in principle, a reason for follow-up contact. These are likely to be low-commitment things such as connecting the person with someone of interest to them or sending some relevant information.
- Move around the room: To avoid becoming stuck, lawyers should have strategies for leaving groups and moving onto others in the room in a polite but assertive manner.

(c) Produce results with follow-up

- Immediately after a networking event, there will be various actions to complete, such as updating the firm's systems and your own, and sharing information with colleagues.
- There should be immediate follow-up of any agreed actions, such as connecting on social media or sending across promised information.
- Lawyers should also take a longer-term view of the next actions to build on any connections they make and add these into their opportunity or sales pipeline systems. Many will continue to develop the initial contacts made with focused content management plans.

A number of books that provide more insight into networking skills are listed in Chapter X of this report.

Generational issues in conversational skills

Chris Hunter was a practising surveyor working in a commercial property development before moving into the legal field. He has been head of business development and marketing at 17-lawyer practice rhw solicitors in Guildford for eight years.

Some of our lawyers are absolutely brilliant – self-motivated and gregarious people who get out there and network. Then there are others who don't understand that generating work involves them at an individual level as well as the firm-wide business development efforts, and rarely want even to go out with clients.

Younger lawyers often have a problem with networking. I blame the demise of the pub culture where, as a teenager, you used to mix with all types of people of different ages and with different backgrounds. You quickly learned the skills of networking and getting on with people. But people don't do that anymore. It's particularly important to know how to develop your own network, as well as rapport and trust – especially if you are a family lawyer and expect people to share information about the most delicate parts of their lives.

Another possible barrier to networking for young lawyers is that they're sometimes dismissive of older people and views that may counter their own; hence the rise of 'zero platforming' attitudes. While the new generation are liberal and way more tolerant of diversity of most types, they can be ageist when it comes to the 'male, pale and stale' people who frequent many business events. Many younger people feel that their working day ends at 6:30pm and are not prepared to devote time in the evenings to networking. Don't even think about asking them to go out to an event that starts at 7:00am!

But maybe this again is because they lack the necessary conversational skills. Young people don't have the same opportunities for early social interaction anymore. The government outlawed opportunities for many of the part-time jobs young folk used to do on an age basis. And many of them don't get work experience, as they fully concentrate on their studies at university. When I scan through 250 CVs for the graduate intake, they are very samey – it's rare to see interesting previous work or life experience. During the first three or four months of their training contract, we often have to spend time preparing them to thrive in the workplace environment.

Face-to-face contact is vital. You can't reach out to people the same way digitally on social media. Some lawyers will take time to write blogs and promote themselves online. They need to be able to understand what clients are likely to want to read – and that's rarely pure technical material, so it takes considerable writing skill. Furthermore, young lawyers now are more likely to use visual social media platforms such as Instagram where there is photo and video sharing, but little interaction beyond 'likes'.

Of course, some firms separate the rainmakers from those lawyers who are purely academic, to be kept in the back room and fed with work. At the other end of the spectrum, those who are close to retirement started their careers in an environment where they were not allowed to promote themselves professionally. That's a hangover cultural issue and can toxify the atmosphere. I often invite younger lawyers who lack confidence to follow me out and shadow my networking for a week or two.

It's not just business development, as the issue can extend to client communication – there have been client concerns that changes to the scope or the fees for work haven't been adequately communicated. Some lawyers may feel they don't want to sully their hands with the commercial sharp end of things. From my experience, many lawyers avoid conflict situations on a personal level.

The problem with being resistant to change and adapting behaviour to get out there and promote themselves is that other professionals – such as accountants – have no such hesitation.

rhw has extensive training and in-house presentations for lawyers, from the first day they join, addressing communication skills and business development. If we can help our staff improve their soft skills, we will.

5.3 Presenting and performing

Lawyers must present at a variety of internal and external events. Public speaking skills can vary significantly between, for example, those needed for formal advocacy in court, for educational and persuasive presentations, and for pitches to prospective clients.

There are two core elements to a good presentation: excellent content that is clear, structured and relevant for the audience; and great delivery so that those listening have a productive and enjoyable experience.

In the marketing and sales context, presenters will want to achieve a specific outcome – for example, to position themselves as the 'go-to' expert on an issue, to initiate a conversation about a particular topic or to get people to sign up for further information.

> *"It is imperative that lawyers produce a marketing plan before they attempt to sell. This will ensure that external environmental and competitor activities, as well as internal skill and resource issues, are understood before a clear value proposition is developed for a specific market."*

Great delivery of presentations requires attention to a number of things, including the following:

- Empathy with the audience: The presenter needs to make a connection with the audience at the outset. This might involve a warm introduction, the creation of an emotional connection through a story or some question or insight that gets the audience onside.
- Signposts and structure: The audience needs to know the purpose of the presentation, what they will gain from it, the journey ahead and where they are in that journey.
- NVC: The speaker will need to inject his or her personality and warmth into the presentation. Most people retain more about how things are said rather than what is actually said. Posture, voice, eye contact, gestures and other non-verbal cues are important.
- Confidence: Familiarity with the material being presented is also important – and this will be affected to some extent by how much the presenter has rehearsed. While notes are an important preparation aid, it can be disconcerting if the presenter spends too much time referring to them.
- Visual aids and props: While visual aids can enhance the experience for the audience, some speakers may be over-reliant on visual aids or use them as an alternative to notes, or simply

read what the audience can see. Presenters can really stand out and be memorable if they use unusual visual aids and props.

- Anecdotes and stories: Lawyers tend to have to present a lot of facts and technical information. Audiences need the presenter to help them understand the information and its relevance. Connection and retention are more likely to be increased where the presenter provides relevant anecdotes and stories.
- Interaction: People have limited attention spans and their concentration will falter after 30 or 40 minutes. So the presenter needs to ensure that there are opportunities for interaction to maintain interest.

There are numerous books to help lawyers present well (see p 172).

5.4 Selling

While the terms 'sales' and 'selling' may be uncomfortable for lawyers, this is a vital skill set if they are to grow their client base, practice and firm. My first book, published back in 2003, tackled the topic of selling for professional services, but was entitled *Dynamic Practice Development*[195] to avoid using the term. To accommodate the advent of social selling, I published a special report called *Social Media in Business Development and Relationship Management: A Guide for Lawyers*[196] in 2018 – again avoiding the use of the term 'selling'.

Too many lawyers adopt a short-term, 'push' approach to selling – they see selling as telling potential clients about their expertise. But telling isn't selling. You need to shift your focus from what you want to sell to what the client might want or need to buy.

It is imperative that lawyers produce a marketing plan before they attempt to sell. This will ensure that external environmental and competitor activities, as well as internal skill and resource issues, are understood before a clear value proposition is developed for a specific market. And the purpose of marketing communications activities is to raise awareness and generate enquiries.

Theodore Levitt[197] said: "Selling focuses on the needs of the seller, marketing on the needs of the buyer. Selling is preoccupied with the seller's need to convert his or her product into cash, marketing with the idea of satisfying the needs of the customer by means of the product and cluster of things associated with creating, delivering and finally consuming it."

Peter Drucker was more concise: "The aim of marketing is to make selling superfluous."[198]

Many law firms adopt a particular framework or methodology to help their lawyers sell more effectively. There are many models around. In the United States, a popular method is Huthwaite International's[199] SPIN® selling; whereas in the United Kingdom, the PACE method[200] is common. Both of these are based on consultative, solutions or problem-solving methodologies; but the latest research suggests that the insight[201] and challenger sales approaches are most effective.

Whatever methodology is adopted, lawyers need the relevant skills to apply within these frameworks. The sales cycle for most complex, technical and commercial services can be significant – years, sometimes – and can involve a lot of people within the decision-making unit. Gartner[202] recently indicated that between six and 10 people are involved in simple B2B buying decisions.

The selling skills that I believe are most important for lawyers include the following:

- Empathy (see p 31): At the heart of effective selling is the need to see things from the client's point of view. Rather than talking about the services provided by the lawyer, the initial conversation should aim to elicit as much information about

"I often reframe selling as 'being more detective', which positions the initial sales process as an investigation to build knowledge of the client and its issues. Being curious about the client, its organisation and sector will inform questions and build empathy."

the personality, style, interests and needs of the other person, so that only information that is relevant is offered.

- Rapport and trust (see p 112): People buy people. And irrational, emotional factors play a major part in the buying process, even for large, sophisticated B2B purchases such as hiring external counsel. The first stage in selling is to establish rapport and trust.
- Adaptation to diversity: Developing rapport and trust requires recognising and adapting to different styles. Clients may have different personalities, gender, cognitive styles, communication preferences, cultural and educational backgrounds. Generational issues may also have an impact.
- Curiosity: I often reframe selling as 'being more detective', which positions the initial sales process as an investigation to build knowledge of the client and its issues. Being curious about the client, its organisation and sector will inform questions and build empathy. Curiosity will drive research that reveals new and unmet client needs. Curiosity will help lawyers to identify opportunities. Curiosity will lead lawyers to challenge current ways of thinking and delivering legal solutions – and drive innovation in the sales process and the services delivered. Curiosity will provide a strong basis for an appropriate solution to both the client's aspirations and afflictions.
- Commerciality: A great lawyer will supplement superb technical legal skills with highly developed commercial nous. Understanding economics, financial and market forces allows the client's problems to be seen through a commercial lens. Clients will need to understand the costs and benefits of any proposed solution, so lawyers need to be attuned and helpful in this. Anticipating the client's commercial needs and finding innovative solutions drive the sales process.
- Add insight and value: The most effective method of selling is the insight or challenger model, where you challenge, inform or educate the person who is buying. This means that lawyers must be equipped with relevant knowledge which becomes a vital ingredient in the value proposition – part of the reason that the client decides to buy. Many law firms invest in developing original content in the form of thought leadership so that their lawyers have access to best practices and innovative ways of thinking about current and emerging issues. I suggest that lawyers find ways to add value – through information or insight – at every interaction with clients during the sales process.
- Problem solving and solutions development: Once a lawyer has uncovered or co-created a client need, he or she must solve the client's problem by developing an appropriate solution. This requires a host of analytical, creative, problem-solving and innovation skills.

- Persuasion: Once the lawyer has identified a problem or opportunity that the client is motivated and able to address, he or she must persuade the client that his or her solution is the best available. There is a huge body of knowledge on the science of persuasion[203] and the hundreds of cognitive biases that affect our decision making.[204] As well as persuasion skills, lawyers must be adept at identifying, classifying and responding to the client's questions and objections.
- Closing and negotiation: At the end of a successful sales process, the lawyer must gain the client's commitment – that is, he or she must close the deal. Agreeing the scope, terms of reference, service standards and fees is an important part of the sales process.

VIII. Soft skills in other professions

It is interesting to see how different professional bodies tackle competencies (or capabilities) and the prominence of soft skills in their professional standard requirements.

1. Solicitors Regulation Authority

The Law Society website says: "To be a successful solicitor you need more than excellent legal knowledge. You must also develop the soft skills you need in your day-to-day work."[205]

CPD was recently replaced with 'continuing competence'. This emphasises reflection and requires solicitors to make an annual declaration of their competence.

1.1 Core competencies

The SRA lists four core competencies:

- ethics, professionalism and judgement;
- technical legal practice;
- working with other people; and
- managing yourself and your own work.

The SRA's competence statement helps you meet the continuing competence requirement.

It recognises the importance of soft skills, such as how to:

- interact with colleagues;
- build and maintain strong relationships with clients; and
- work effectively as part of a team.

The threshold standard sets the minimum level of competence needed for solicitors to continue to practise. This is set at Level 3, which is also the standard at which someone qualifying as a solicitor would be expected to perform.

1.2 Professional Skills Course

The PSC core modules cover:

- advocacy and communication skills;
- client care and professional standards; and
- financial and business skills.

The Solicitors Qualifying Examination will introduce a common assessment that all solicitors will take before qualifying and is set to be introduced in Autumn 2021.

1.3 Practice Skills Standards

These are the Practice Skills Standards for trainee solicitors, which blend soft skills with technical skills:

- advocacy and oral presentation;
- dispute resolution;
- case and transaction management;
- communication;
- establishing and maintaining professional relationships;
- drafting;
- interviewing and advising;
- legal research;
- negotiation;
- ethics, professionalism and judgement; and
- managing themselves and their own work.

2. Institute of Chartered Accountants in England and Wales

There are two qualifications for accountants: the associated chartered accountant qualification is for those who would like to pursue a career in auditing and accounting; whereas the Association of Certified Chartered Accountant qualification is more comprehensive, giving options to pursue a career in management accounting, financial management and financial services.

The seven professional developments skills for students are:

- adding value;
- communication;
- decision making;
- ethics and professionalism;
- problem solving;
- teamwork; and
- technical competence.

The soft skills section of the Institute of Chartered Accountants in England and Wales (ICAEW)[206] website explores its leadership development programme.

According to the 2019 Sage *Practice of Now*[207] report, US accountancy firms cite soft skills as their number one priority. Of the 3,000 accountants surveyed in the report, 90% believe there has been a cultural shift in accountancy as it enters the third decade of the 21st century. This shift is driving significant changes in hiring practices, business services and attitudes towards emerging technologies across the globe. The report revealed that 49% of respondents had formally examined their business practices in the last year, with an additional 26% doing so over the last five years.

"To bring the accounting profession to the future, accountants need to embrace the technology and training that will ultimately allow them to expand into a more consultative role. US accounting firms no longer have the luxury of time. They need to adopt new technology and business models today, or risk being left behind."

"As evidenced in the *Practice of Now* report, many US accountants would like to offer more advisory and consulting services, but feel they lack the necessary time or skills to do so," said Jennifer Warawa, EVP of Partners, Accountants and Alliances, at Sage. "To bring the accounting profession to the future, accountants need to embrace the technology and training that will ultimately allow them to expand into a more consultative role. US accounting firms no longer have the luxury of time. They need to adopt new technology and business models today, or risk being left behind."

One mid-tier accountancy firm had a new manager pathway programme – which it opened to clients as well as staff – that adopted the following model for management training:

- managing self;
- managing others;
- managing teams;
- motivation;
- communication;
- managing conflict; and
- managing your impact.

Global accountancy firm PwC's Whole Leadership Award[208] covers the following:

- technical capabilities (the ability to create value for clients and PwC);
- business acumen (the ability to bring business knowledge and awareness);
- global acumen (a global mind-set that goes beyond borders);
- relationships (the ability to build genuine, trust-based relationships); and
- whole leadership (the ability to lead, make a difference and deliver results).

The ICAEW recently introduced the Developing Leadership in Practice[209] programme for new and aspiring partners. It develops the following leadership skills: commercial awareness, client service, relationship building, problem solving and the ability to secure positive outcomes, effective communication and team collaboration.

3. Royal Institution of Chartered Surveyors

Trainee surveyors must complete an assessment of professional confidence to qualify.

The Royal Institution of Chartered Surveyors (RICS) competencies[210] are in three distinct categories:

- mandatory – the personal, interpersonal, professional practice and business skills common to all pathways and mandatory for all candidates;
- technical core – the primary skills of the chosen pathway; and
- technical optional – additional skills requirements for each pathway from a list of competencies relevant to the area of practice.

Each competency is defined at three levels of attainment:

- Level 1 – knowledge and understanding:
  - accounting principles and procedures;
  - business planning;
  - conflict avoidance, management and dispute resolution procedures;
  - data management;
  - diversity, inclusion and team working;
  - inclusive environments; and
  - sustainability.

- Level 2 – application of knowledge:
  - client care;
  - communication and negotiation; and
  - health and safety.

- Level 3 – reasoned advice, depth and synthesis of technical knowledge and its implementation:
  - ethics, rules of conduct and professionalism.

Senior Professional Assessment:

- Level 2:
  - leadership; and
  - managing people

IX. Concluding observations

So what conclusions may be drawn made from the (admittedly limited) set of interviews conducted in the research for this report – albeit within the context of 30 years working with lawyers to develop their practices and soft skills?

1. The growing importance of soft skills

Beyond and within the legal profession, recognition of the importance of soft skills is growing. Soft skills are crucial to support client service excellence; to differentiate; to attract and retain the best talent; to ensure great client relationships; to manage constant change successfully; and to carve out a secure place in the face of the imminent threat of automation and AI.

However, the appetite and ability to respond to this urgent need vary significantly among law firms.

2. A wide variety of soft skills are needed by modern lawyers

The research confirms beyond doubt that the range of soft skills required by modern lawyers is wide and growing. While most law firms know what good soft skills look like when they see them, there is still considerable confusion about precisely what those skills and attributes are and how best to develop them.

While most law firms are clear on the technical competencies that lawyers need at different levels of seniority, few can articulate the soft skills needed with the same precision and confidence.

Furthermore, while the larger law firms have greater access to the expertise and resources needed to introduce structured and integrated programmes of soft skills development, it is likely that the need for those soft skills will be most acute in smaller firms, which perhaps cannot compete on the automation front.

3. Greater need for leadership skills
In today's challenging, fast-changing environment, the legal profession needs great leadership. Some firms differentiate between leadership and other soft skills training, while others take a more integrated approach.

However, I would argue that too many firms reserve leadership training for a small minority of those who will be running firms, departments or offices; whereas in fact these skills are needed throughout the organisation. Leadership skills should be developed from the very beginning of a legal career.

4. The role of professional bodies
Business schools and medical schools have integrated soft skills training into admissions and curricula. The initial training undertaken by lawyers should similarly be revised to incorporate soft skills. This must be led by the Law Society. The Legal Education and Training Group,[211] I believe, is pressing for change.

Professional bodies could also lead the way in defining soft skill competency frameworks for lawyers, to prevent each firm from having to reinvent the wheel and ensure consistent basic standards across the profession.

Professional bodies can also play a valuable role in developing high-quality training programmes which all lawyers – regardless of the size and resources of their firms – can access. The Law Society of Ireland has excellent programmes[212] on growth strategies, leadership development and coaching skills, and also offers a certificate in professional training to equip lawyers to teach. The ICAEW's partner leadership programme is another good example.

5. Emotional intelligence is critical
Empathy and the ability to read other people and adjust behaviour accordingly underpin many of the soft skills required by lawyers.

The importance of EQ – particularly in communication, client service delivery and business development – is apparent. Yet the psychometric tools to measure this ability do not appear to be used much during the assessment, development and promotion of lawyers. It is hard to discern which firms are dedicating resources to developing the EQ of their lawyers.

6. Under-developed business development skills

Most of those interviewed felt that their lawyers needed to develop more human skills to support their business development effectiveness – whether this was in communication, networking, relationship building or selling.

But the evidence suggests that this is often tackled in a piecemeal, ad hoc way, without a structured approach to identify the overall competencies required at each stage of a legal career or when lawyers engage in their firm's business development programmes.

7. The jury is out on digital training

A few firms have started to explore digital training methods – although typically this is for knowledge dissemination on regulatory topics such as anti-money laundering, cybersecurity and mental health awareness.

The jury appears to be out on the value of digital training in developing soft skills, although blended learning and activity-based learning were mentioned. However, the recent public health restrictions as a result of the coronavirus pandemic may accelerate interest and investment in, and development and adoption of, e-learning. Alternatively, it may further highlight the limitations of such platforms.

Where e-learning has been embraced, there appears to be excellent use of neuroscience and sophisticated learning technology to identify learners' individual styles and preferences, and tailor digital learning interactions accordingly.

8. Greater use of coaching

Many firms continue to adopt traditional methods of training, through classroom and workshop-based learning environments. But it was interesting to see so many firms talk about their increasing use of coaching – through both the use of external, professionally qualified coaches and the development of coaching skills throughout their leadership and management teams.

Coaching is emerging as a core skill – in particular, to help motivation, practise new skills and embed behaviour as part of cultural change programmes.

"While the larger law firms have greater access to the expertise and resources needed to introduce structured and integrated programmes of soft skills development, it is likely that the need for those soft skills will be most acute in smaller firms, which perhaps cannot compete on the automation front."

9. Globalisation driving the need for cross-cultural competency

For larger firms, cross-cultural competency will become increasingly important, although there was little evidence of soft skills development in this area. Hopefully we will see more firms embrace cross-cultural and diversity skills training, to take advantage of global talent.

10. The future?

Much training within law firms remains focused on technical legal knowledge and skills. In many situations, soft skills development is either a recent development or an optional, *ad hoc* addition to established training programmes. And in many firms, there seems to be a tick-box approach to soft skills training, underpinned by the view that a few hours is adequate to develop complex, high-level soft skills.

Yet much of the research on future employment trends points to the need for skills beyond those reliant on intellectual capability and technical know-how – which will be absorbed by dramatic advances in AI and machine learning. Human skills will be in demand and at a premium. This point is argued brilliantly by Greg Orme.[213]

While many firms will continue to invest in new business models and the use of technology to improve efficiency and develop innovative new services, others will look to the soft skills of their lawyers to drive their differentiation strategies. Ideally, firms should embrace both opportunities – before they become threats.

X. Signposts to other learning resources

There are many resources addressing soft skills in general and in particular for lawyers. I have selected my favourite books, those mentioned during interviews and the most popular in the business community, and would appreciate feedback and additions to build the list further in the future.

1. Recommended books

Topic	Title	Author(s)	Publisher/ edition	Notes
Change management	*The Change Catalyst: Secrets to Successful and Sustainable Business Change*	Campbell MacPherson	2017 John Wiley & Sons	A comprehensive and practical guide to business change management.
	Switch: How to Change Things When Change Is Hard	Chip and Dan Heath	2011 Random House	A quick but worthy read with interesting case studies of social change.
	Making Sense of Change Management: A Complete Guide to the Models, Tools and Techniques of Organisational Change	Esther Cameron and Mike Green	2015 Kogan Page	More academic, but comprehensive coverage of change models, tools and techniques.
	Neuroscience of Organizational Change: An Evidence-Based Practical Guide to Managing Change	Hilary Scarlett	2016 Kogan Page	An evidence-based practical guide.
Coaching and mentoring	*Helping People Change: Coaching with Compassion for Lifelong Learning and Growth*	Richard Boyatzis, Melvin Smith and Ellen Van Oosten	2019 Harvard Business Review Press	An evidence-based book on intentional change theory.
	Key Coaching Models: The 70+ Models Every Manager and Coach Needs to Know	Stephen Gribben	2016 FT Publishing International	A compendium of over 70 models for use by coaching professionals.
	Coaching and Mentoring: Practical Methods To Improve Learning	Eric Parsloe and Monika Wray	2001 Kogan Page	A great introduction – Eric was my personal tutor when I qualified as a coach.
Conflict management	*Conversational Riffs: Creating Meaning Out of Conflict*	Neil Denny	2010 Eldamar Ltd	From a family mediator's perspective using a music metaphor.
	Emotional Intelligence: Dealing with Difficult People	Various	2018 Harvard Business Review Emotional Intelligence series	Short introduction including hot or cold conflicts, stress, urgency and passive aggressive behaviour.
Consulting	*Flawless Consulting: A Guide to Getting Your Expertise Used*	Peter Block	2011 John Wiley & Sons 3rd edition	Once adopted by the leading management consultancy practices.
Delegation	*Deep and Deliberate Delegation: A New Art for Unleashing Talent and Winning Back Time*	Dave Stitt	2018 21CPL Productions	A recent addition to the many books on delegation.

continued on next page

Topic	Title	Author(s)	Publisher/ edition	Notes
Diversity	*Rebel Ideas: The Power of Diverse Thinking*	Matthew Syed	2019 John Murray	Strongly recommended to me.
Emotional intelligence	*Emotional Intelligence 2.0*	Travis Bradberry and Jean Greaves	2009 TalentSmart	Introduces the four core areas and includes an online assessment.
	Emotional Intelligence: Why It Can Matter More Than IQ	Daniel Goleman	1996 Bloomsbury Publishing Ltd	One of the first books on the subject.
Influence	*How to Win Friends and Influence People*	Dale Carnegie	2004 Vermilion 28 edition	An old (1930s) but excellent book on building relationships, influence and selling.
	Key Person of Influence: The Five-Step Method to Become One of the Most Highly Valued and Highly Paid People in Your Industry	Daniel Priestley	2014 Rethink Press Revised edition	Process for building your personal brand.
Leadership	*Professional Services Leadership Handbook: How to Lead a Professional Services Firm in a New Age of Competitive Disruption*	Nigel Clark, Ben Kent, Alastair Beddow and Adrian Furner	2017 Kogan Page	Excellent book written for leaders in professional services firms.
	Effective Leadership: How to Be a Successful Leader	John Adair	2009 Pan	John Adair has written many books on leadership.
	Good to Great: Why Some Companies Make The Leap... And Others Don't	Jim Collins	2001 Random House Business	A best-selling classic on leading businesses from good to great performance.
Management	*Visionary Leadership in A Turbulent World – Thriving In The New VUCA Context*	Editors: Rob Elkington Madeleine van der Steege Judith Glick-Smith Jennifer Moss Breen	2017 Emerald Publishing	Managing with volatility, uncertainty, complexity and ambiguity.
	The New One Minute Manager	Ken Blanchard, Spencer Johnson	2015 Harper	Some original helpful tips.

continued on next page

Topic	Title	Author(s)	Publisher/ edition	Notes
Marketing and business development	*The Legal PR Guide*	PRCA/Byfield Consultancy	2019 Free guide available here: http://byfieldconsultancy.com/2019/11/prca-legal-pr-guide/	Multiple contributors on a range of topics – a free guide published in 2019.
	The Thought Leadership Manual: How to Grab Your Clients' Attention With Powerful Ideas	Tim Prizeman	2015 Panoma Press	A brilliantly practical, must-read from a communications professional who has worked with the professions for decades.
	Rainmakers and Trailblazers: A Practical Step-By-Step Guide to Effective Business Development By Lawyers	Kim Tasso	2014 Worldwide Legal Research Ltd	Part one from an individual lawyer perspective and part two from the firm and practice group viewpoint.
	Marketing the Professional Services Firm: Applying the Principles of Marketing to the Professions	Laurie Young	2005 John Wiley & Sons	The original book on the topic and adopted as the course text for professional services marketing qualifications.
	Professional Services Marketing Handbook: How to Build Relationships, Grow Your Firm and Become a Client Champion	Edited by Nigel Clark with Charles Nixon	2015 Kogan Page	Plenty of case studies included – particularly of law firms, but aimed at marketing professionals.
Mediation	*The Definitive Guide To Workplace Mediation And Managing Conflict At Work*	Clive Lewis OBE	2009 Roper Penberthy Publishing Ltd	A solid introduction for human resources.
	Mediation Skills and Strategies: A Practical Guide	Tony Whatling	2012 Jessica Kingsley Publishers	An introduction for mediators.
Mental health	*Lost Connections: Why You're Depressed and How to Find Hope*	Johann Hari	2018 Bloomsbury	The nine causes of depression and mental health guidance.
	The Chimp Paradox: The Acclaimed Mind Management Programme to Help You Achieve Success, Confidence and Happiness	Dr Steve Peters	2012 Vermilion	Conquer your fears and operate with control, focus and confidence.
	Crazy Busy – Overstretched, Overbooked and About To Snap! Strategies for Handling Your Fast-Paced Life	Edward M Hallowell MD	2007 Ballentine Books	An incredibly forward-thinking look at the impact of digital society – and pragmatic solutions for avoiding stress.

continued on next page

Topic	Title	Author(s)	Publisher/ edition	Notes
Negotiation	*The Leader's Guide to Negotiation: How to Use Soft Skills to Get Hard Results*	Simon Horton	2016 FT Publishing International	Excellent book providing an overview of negotiation with an emphasis on soft skills.
	Getting to Yes: Negotiating an Agreement Without Giving In	Roger Fisher and William Ury	1999 Random House Business Books Second edition	Key ideas and practical techniques.
Networking	*How To Be Great at the Stuff You Hate: The Straight-Talking Guide to Networking, Persuading and Selling*	Nick Davies	2011 Capstone	Written by a former barrister.
	Business Networking – The Survival Guide: How To Make Networking Less About Stress and More about Success	Will Kintish	2014 Pearson Business	Written by a former accountant.
NVC	*Body Language: How to Read Others' Thoughts by their Gestures (Overcoming Common Problems)*	Allan Pearse and John Chandler	1997 Sheldon Press	An introduction to NVC.
	Body Language at Work	Adrian Furnham	1999 Chartered Institute of Personnel & Development	A short introduction to workplace NVC.
Personal effectiveness	*The 7 Habits Of Highly Effective People*	Stephen R Covey	2004 Simon and Schuster	Reprinted Edition The seven habits are: • Be proactive. • Begin with the end in mind. • Put first things first. • Think win-win. • Seek first to understand then to be understood. • Synergise. • Sharpen the saw.
Persuasion	*Influence: The Psychology of Persuasion*	Dr Robert B Cialdini	2007 Harper Business Revised edition	Explores the six key drivers of persuasion from a psychology and marketing expert.
Presentations	*HBR Guide to Persuasive Presentations*	Nancy Duarte	2012 Harvard Business Review Press	Excellent introduction.
	TED Talks: The Official TED Guide to Public Speaking	Chris Anderson	2016 Headline	From the founder of TED.
	The Presentation Book	Emma Ledden	2017 Pearson Business 2 edition	Entertaining and helpful.

continued on next page

Topic	Title	Author(s)	Publisher/ edition	Notes
Profession-alism	*True Professionalism: The Courage to Care about Your People, Your Clients, and Your Career*	David H Maister,	1997 The Free Press	A respected book.
	The Trusted Advisor	David H Maister, Robert Galford, Charles W Green	2000 Simon & Schuster Ltd	Original work on trust in relationships in the professions.
Psychology	*Nudge: Improving Decisions about Health, Wealth and Happiness*	Richard Thaler and Cass Sunstein	2008 Yale University Press	An exploration of unconscious forces such as emotion and cognitive biases and designing choice architectures to 'nudge' better decisions.
	The Choice Factory: 25 Behavioural Biases that Influence What We Buy	Richard Shotton	2018 Harriman House	Key behavioural biases.
	Lateral Thinking	Edward de Bono	1986 Hazel Watson & Viney Ltd Ninth edition	An early text supporting creative thinking.
	NLP – The New Technology of Achievement	Steve Andreas and Charles Faulkner	1997 Positive Paperbacks Third edition	One of the first books on NLP.
Relationships	*Better Business Relationships*	Kim Tasso	2019 Bloomsbury	A variety of soft skills in the DACRIE model – diversity, adaptation and learning, communications, relationships, internal relationships (team building), external relationships (selling)
	Effective Client Management in Professional Services: How To Build Successful Client Relationships	Jack Berkovi	2014 Gower	A good introduction to client management for lawyers.
Selling	*Insight Selling*	Mike Schultz and John E Doerr	2014 John Wiley & Sons	For those experienced in selling – introduces the challenger model of selling.
	Dynamic Practice Development: Selling Skills For Professionals	Kim Tasso	2003 Thorogood (Original version printed in 2000).	My first book on selling in the professions which provides an introduction to selling.
	Spin® Selling	Neil Rackham	1996 Gower Publishing Ltd Reprint	Psychology-based sales methodology. Popular with US law firms.

continued on next page

Topic	Title	Author(s)	Publisher/ edition	Notes
Selling *continued*	*Smarter Selling: Next Generation Sales Strategies to Meet Your Buyer's Needs – Every Time*	Keith Dugdale and David Lambert	2007 Pearson Education Ltd	A simple, entry-level introduction to selling.
	The New Strategic Selling: The Unique Sales System Proven Successful by the World's Best Companies	Stephen H Heiman, Diane Sanchez with Tad Tuleja	1998 Kogan Page Third Edition	Another key sales methodology.
Social media	*Social Media in Business Development and Relationship Management: A Guide For Lawyers*	Kim Tasso	2018 Globe Law and Business	The pros and cons of social media for lawyers and law firms, and step-by-step guides on using LinkedIn, Facebook and Twitter.
Soft skills	*Soft Skills for the Effective Lawyer*	Randall Kiser	2017 Cambridge University Press	An in-depth, technical and academic review of soft skills for US attorneys.
	The Human Edge: How Curiosity and Creativity are Your Superpowers in The Digital Economy	Greg Orme	2019 Pearson Business	Consciousness, curiosity, creativity and collaboration. Using human skills in response to the threat of AI.
Tendering	*Strategic Tendering for Professional Services*	Matthew Fuller and Tim Nightingale	2017 Kogan Page	A brilliant and comprehensive book written by professional services experts.
Thinking	*Time to Think: Listening to Ignite the Human Mind*	Nancy Kline	2002 Cassell	Creating an appreciative environment
Writing	*Persuasive Writing: How to Harness the Power of Words*	Peter Frederick	2011 Pearson Business	One of my favourite books
	Business Writing: How to Write to Engage, Persuade and Sell	Ian Atkinson	2011 Financial Times/ Prentice Hall	Excellent introduction to business writing basics.
Other	*Range: How Generalists Triumph in a Specialized World*	David Epstein	2019 Macmillan	An interesting perspective.
	Reinforcements: How to Get People to Help You	Heidi Grant	2018 Harvard Business Review Press	The psychology of getting people to help you – with pragmatic advice.

2. Training organisations

There are many training organisations providing soft skills training for lawyers in the United Kingdom, although some only extend their training to their members. I have named some of the best known in Table 8.

Table 8. Soft skills training organisations

Central Law Training	www.clt.co.uk/eng/
Law Society of Ireland	www.lawsociety.ie/Courses—Events/cpd/FinuasSkillnet/
LawNet	www.lawnet.co.uk/membership-benefits/learning-development/
LawSouth	www.lawsouth.co.uk/#login
LETG	http://letg.org.uk/
Managing Partners Forum	www.mpfglobal.com/
MBL	www.mblseminars.com/
OpenLearn	www.open.edu/openlearn/
QDooz	https://qdooz.com/
TED	www.ted.com/
The Law Society	www.lawsociety.org.uk/support-services/education-learning/

Appendix I. Illustrative competency dictionary and framework

Illustrative competency dictionary (Table 1)

This illustrative competency dictionary was provided by Sue Colton, director and founder of SJC Consulting.

Generic competencies	
Passion for excellence	Displaying the drive to be nothing but the best.
Professional expertise	Delivering and upholding outstanding performance as a recognised expert in the appropriate field.
Client care and commitment	Effectively building and maintaining trusted relationships valued by clients.
Information gathering	Seeking and sharing the right breadth and depth of accurate and relevant information.
Problem solving	Finding the best relevant solution and outcome for both the client and the practice.
Decision making	Making sure all relevant information is obtained in order to make effective decisions.
Service delivery	Being conscientious and driven in delivering results for the client, the practice and the teams.
Communication	Conveying a strong personal impression through every appropriate communication mechanism.
Team working	Displaying team allegiance and direction that support and maintain our valued culture.
Leadership competencies	
Building capability	Increasing the capability of the team and the practice.
Business acumen and vision	Aligning technical knowledge and complex business understanding to formulate and drive strategic vision.
Influencing and leveraging relationships	Naturally building bonds with others which generate mutual trust, respect, confidence, collaboration and support.
Inspiring and motivating	Being an example of energy and integrity; engaging and invigorating people and supporting their belief in themselves.

Competency assessment criteria (Table 2)

Generic competency	Professional expertise Delivering outstanding performance as a recognised expert in my appropriate field
Competency Level 3	• I ensure that my professional knowledge/expertise is the most up to date and I am aware of impending changes and developments, being able to disseminate the relevant technical and legislative frameworks articulately and accurately to others. • My advice is trusted by people in my business and within my profession. • I am continually proactive in my relevant wider business community, and seek positions of importance within relevant external bodies and committees. • I am a mentor to others around my business and seek out coaching opportunities, as well as professional input from others when required. • I am renowned for embedding a culture that ensures that internal quality is consistently applied, and that we adhere to all required protocols and standards.
Competency Level 2	• I am recognised as having professional credibility throughout my business. • I willingly and appropriately involve other experts when offering professional opinions and solutions, to ensure the broadest perspective is achieved. • I seek ways to broaden my technical knowledge and increase my professional standing. • I strive to ensure that the professional advice I give is technically, ethically and legally sound and up to date. • I am fully aware of the risks associated with my role and anticipate and mitigate for any that may arise.
Competency Level 1	• Others trust my technical expertise and integrity when they request my input. • I am keen to own and expand my professional and technical skills by pursuing relevant knowledge-sharing opportunities and identifying role models within the business and profession, undertaking CPD activities as appropriate to my job and profession. • I am able to express my concern when I feel the risks are too great. • I recognise when further professional opinion should be sought. • I operate within professional, ethical and legal boundaries, while positively projecting, protecting and nurturing the reputation of the business.
Competency Level 0	• I see little opportunity for professional development and may overlook chances to learn from others. • I sometimes ignore obvious risks when decision making and may disregard others' caution without giving due consideration to their concerns. • I miss opportunities to promote the business. • The quality and accuracy of information I provide is often questioned. • I rarely seek input from others and prefer to work alone.

Appendix II. Example RICS mandatory competency

Communications and negotiation

Description of competency in context of this sector

This competency covers the way in which a surveyor communicates, in writing, graphically and orally. It also looks at the process and strategy of a negotiation. Effective communication is a fundamental aspect of professionalism and candidates must be able to communicate complex technical matters to both technical and non-technical people in a clear fashion. Negotiation is a regular part of a surveyor's work and this competency deals with taking a systematic approach to achieving a satisfactory conclusion.

Examples of likely knowledge, skills and experience at each level

Level 1
Demonstrate knowledge and understanding of effective oral, written, graphic and presentation skills including the methods and techniques that are appropriate to specific situations.
Examples of knowledge comprised within this level are: • Good grammar and spelling • The etiquette of written communication in emails, letters and reports • Common formats for reports • Presentation of figures and data using spreadsheets, graphs and charts • How to deliver a report at a meeting • How to structure and deliver a presentation • Establishing your objectives and strategy for a negotiation • The process of negotiation
Level 2
Provide evidence of practical application of oral, written, graphic and presentation skills that are appropriate in a variety of situations, specifically including where negotiation is involved.
Examples of activities and knowledge comprised within this level are: • Writing letters or other formal documents • Compiling a report • Compiling minutes of meetings • Producing pricing documents • Delivering reports at meetings • Taking part in interviews, eg, for contractor selection • Giving presentations to staff or project teams • Negotiating a loss and expense claim, extension of time, acceleration programme, contract sum or final account • Agreeing the value of an instruction

continued on next page

Level 3
Provide evidence of evaluation of your communication in a variety of situations.
Examples of activities and knowledge comprised within this level are: • Issuing reports to clients • Producing in-house management communications • Chairing meetings • Conducting interviews • Presenting at seminars • Public speaking on behalf of your business • Agreement of fees with a client • Advising on complex negotiations or disputes, eg, claims for loss and expense

Source: © RICS Requirements and Competencies Guide

Notes

1 Dale Carnegie attributed this to Roosevelt in newspaper columns in 1939 and 1942, but a direct quote has not been found in a citation during Roosevelt's lifetime.
2 Ian Pearson, *Work – A Futurizon Report*, December 2008, https://unions21.org.uk/files/The-Future-of-Work[1].pdf.
3 Seth Godin, *It's Your Turn*, 31 January 2017, https://itsyourturnblog.com/lets-stop-calling-them-soft-skills-9cc27ec09ecb.
4 Pearson, n 2.
5 *Macmillan Dictionary.*
6 http://disco-tools.eu/disco2_portal/.
7 RJ Sternberg, *Beyond IQ: A Triarchic Theory of Intelligence* (Cambridge University Press 1985).
8 Malcolm Gladwell, *Outliers: The Story of Success* (Penguin 2009).
9 Raymond R Reilly and Gregory P Reilly, "Building Business Acumen", *HR West*, December 2009.
10 https://en.wikipedia.org/wiki/Soft_skills.
11 Dale Carnegie, *How to Win Friends and Influence People* (World's Work Ltd 1975).
12 Hugo Brit, "Can We Agree to Stop Calling Them 'Soft Skills'?", Procurious, 18 August 2016, www.procurious.com/procurement-news/stop-calling-soft-skills.
13 *Ibid.*
14 Brit, n 12.
15 "The hard truth about soft skills", American Management Association, 24 January 2019, www.amanet.org/articles/the-hard-truth-about-soft-skills/. These statistics were extrapolated from Charles Riborg Mann, *A Study of Engineering Education* (Carnegie Foundation 1918).
16 World Economic Forum, *The Future of Jobs Report 2018*, 17 September 2018, https://fr.weforum.org/reports/the-future-of-jobs-report-2018.
17 Avil Beckford, "The skills you need to succeed in 2020", *Forbes*, 6 August 2018, www.forbes.com/sites/ellevate/2018/08/06/the-skills-you-need-to-succeed-in-2020/#5a507e4288a0.
18 Ellen Van Velsor and Joel Wright, "Expanding the leadership equation – Developing next-generation leaders", Center for Creative Leadership, October 2012, www.ccl.org/wp-content/uploads/2015/04/ExpandingLeadershipEquation.pdf.
19 Warren Berger, "Why Curious People Are Destined for the C-Suite", *Harvard Business Review*, 11 September 2015, https://hbr.org/2015/09/why-curious-people-are-destined-for-the-c-suite.
20 Deloitte Insights from IMPACT 2018, Bersin Insights Team, www2.deloitte.com/content/dam/Deloitte/ca/Documents/audit/ca-audit-abm-scotia-insights-from-impact-2018.pdf.
21 Tomas Chamorro-Premuzic and Becky Frankiewicz," Does Higher Education Still Prepare People for Jobs?", *Harvard Business Review*, 14 January 2019, https://hbr.org/2019/01/does-higher-education-still-prepare-people-for-jobs.
22 https://qdooz.com/.
23 Amanda Van Nuys, "New LinkedIn Research: Upskill your employees with the skills companies need most in 2020", LinkedIn, 28 December 2019, https://learning.linkedin.com/blog/learning-thought-leadership/most-in-demand-skills-2020.
24 Jacob Morgan, "140 Top CEOs Identify Crucial Skills and Mindsets for Future Leaders", LinkedIn, 24 February 2020, www.linkedin.com/pulse/140-top-ceos-identify-crucial-skills-mindsets-future-leaders-morgan/.
25 Cited in Randall Kiser, *Beyond Right and Wrong: The Power of Effective Decision Making for Attorneys and Clients* (Springer 2014).
26 SRA, Legal Ombudsman and London Economics, *Research into the experiences and effectiveness of solicitors' first tier complaints handling processes*, October 2017
27 "Why lawyers need to develop soft skills", *Solicitors Journal*, March 2019.
28 Randall Kiser, *Soft Skills for the Effective Lawyer* (Cambridge University Press 2017).
29 Chaaya R Jugdeb, "Soft skills that set great lawyers apart from the rest", *The Counsel Network*, 24 April 2018.
30 Mark A Cohen, "What's a lawyer now? Law's shift from practice to skill", *Forbes*, 23 September 2019.
31 Sonica Mouton, "Developing Soft Skills for Future Lawyers", Futures Law Faculty, 8 March 2019, www.futureslawfaculty.online/post/developing-soft-skills-for-future-lawyers.
32 Suan Smith Blakely, "Law Firms Shouldn't Overlook Value of Soft Skills", *ABA Journal*, 7 March 2019, www.abajournal.com/voice/article/law-firms-shouldnt-overlook-the-value-of-soft-skills.
33 www.prospects.ac.uk/jobs-and-work-experience/job-sectors/law-sector/7-skills-for-a-successful-law-career.
34 Greg Orme, *The Human Edge: How Curiosity and Creativity are Your Superpowers in the Digital Economy* (Pearson 2019).
35 LexisNexis, *The Good Solicitor's Skill Set*, The Bellwether Report Series 2019, www.lexisnexis.co.uk/research-and-reports/bellwether-2019-the-good-solicitors-skill-set-bd.html.
36 Paul Hodkinson, "Technology Means Lawyers Are Losing the Human Touch", *UK Legal Week*, www.law.com/international-edition/2020/01/16/technology-is-limiting-the-depth-of-lawyer-client-relationships-378-132105/?slreturn=20200321065207.
37 David Guest, "The Hunt is on for the Renaissance Man of Computing", *The Independent*, 17 September 1991.

38 R Amani Smathers, "T-Shaped Lawyer", 17 September, 2019
39 David Expstein, *Range: How Generalists Triumph in the Specialised World* (Macmillan 2019).
40 Dan Kayne, *Chapter 2: The Lawyer of the Future* webinar, www.apperio.com/video/chapter-2-the-lawyer-of-the-future/.
41 Natalie Runyon, Alyson Carrel, Cat Moon, Shellie Reid and Gabe Teninbaum, "The Delta Model: Simple, Accurate, Versatile", *Legal Revolution*, 10 November 2019, www.legalevolution.org/2019/11/the-delta-model-simple-accurate-versatile-125/.
42 Sarah O'Connor, "The robot-proof skills that give women an edge in the age of AI", *Financial Times*, 11 February 2019, www.ft.com/content/06afd24a-2dfb-11e9-ba00-0251022932c8
43 Travis Bradberry and Jean Greaves, *Emotional Intelligence 2.0* (TalentSmart 2009).
44 *Ibid.*
45 *Ibid.*
46 *Ibid.*
47 *Ibid.*
48 *Ibid.*
49 *Ibid.*
50 *Ibid.*
51 Tasha Eurich, "Working with People Who Aren't Self-Aware", *Harvard Business Review*, 19 October 2018, https://hbr.org/2018/10/working-with-people-who-arent-self-aware.
52 Travis Bradberry and Jean Greaves, *Emotional Intelligence 2.0* (TalentSmart 2009).
53 The Myers-Briggs Company, "MBTI® – the Myers-Briggs Type Indicator", https://eu.themyersbriggs.com/en/tools/MBTI?gclid=CjwKCAjwnIr1BRAWEiwA6GpwNftc9I7BTxnPGTbgUz5jbW72dYp-ZXi2Qx9sBclkool8NCViob2ZfBoCmiMQAvD_BwE.
54 "Insights Discovery Colour Energies: A Beginners Guide", The Colour Works, www.thecolourworks.com/insights-discovery-colour-types-guide/.
55 www2.deloitte.com/uk/en/pages/operations/solutions/business-chemistry.html#.
56 www.hoganassessments.com/assessments/.
57 Daniel Goleman, 12 June 2017, www.danielgoleman.info/three-kinds-of-empathy-cognitive-emotional-compassionate/.
58 Shawn Christopher Shea, *Psychiatric Interviewing: The Art of Understanding – A Practical Guide for Psychiatrists, Psychologists, Counselors, Social Workers, Nurses, and Other Professionals* (Elsevier 2016).
59 *Emotional Intelligence* series, *Harvard Business Review*, https://store.hbr.org/product/hbr-emotional-intelligence-ultimate-boxed-set-14-books-hbr-emotional-intelligence-series/10377 14 books in a box set.
60 Jean Hartley, "Political astuteness: an essential workplace skill", *HR Magazine*, 6 July 2015, www.hrmagazine.co.uk/article-details/political-astuteness-an-essential-workplace-skill-1.
61 "Brené Brown on why courage, vulnerabilty and authenticity have to be practiced" – an excerpt from *ORIGIN* magazine, Huffpost, www.huffpost.com/entry/brene-brown-origin-magazine-interview_n_3796923?guccounter=1&guce_referrer=aHRocHM6Ly93d3cuZ29vZ2xlLmNvbS8&guce_referrer_sig=AQAAAGPxZUwNoaVdzjSGIZtJ7uGv64kuWQki_SGmB-onJjLXayLkoo_opiTCLEZ6lhTo3iXoqqGvOqk1Qwlv-6bK8Pi6LvZJwTSMFRdN_oXYofrKaklESdOhlZZIkReVIZBoUEQa_aomQioXuSsMjhXBeJonTEQu8AEbweT-p256tG9H.
62 Diane Coutu, "How Resilience Works", *Harvard Business Review*, May 2002, https://hbr.org/2002/05/how-resilience-works.
63 Dan Siegel and David Rock, "The Healthy Mind Platter", www.drdansiegel.com/resources/healthy_mind_platter/.
64 Center for Creative Leadership, "A Leader's Best Bet: Exercise", www.ccl.org/articles/leading-effectively-articles/spotlight-on-exercise-and-leadership/.
65 Coutu, n 62.
66 For example, Richard H Thaler and Cass R Sunstein, *Nudge: Improving Decisions About Health, Wealth and Happiness* (Penguin 2009).
67 John Tierney, "Do You Suffer from Decision Fatigue?" *New York Times*, 17 August 2011, www.nytimes.com/2011/08/21/magazine/do-you-suffer-from-decision-fatigue.html.
68 David Cresswell, "Distraction: A Good Thing" Carnegie Mellon University 2013, www.cmu.edu/homepage/health/2013/spring/distraction-a-good-thing.shtml.
69 https://psychology.nd.edu/faculty/jessica-payne/.
70 Steve Glaveski, "Where Companies Go Wrong with Learning and Development", *Harvard Business Review*, 2 October 2019, https://hbr.org/2019/10/where-companies-go-wrong-with-learning-and-development.
71 Loizis Heracleous and Jachen Wirtz, "The Globe: Singapore Airlines' Balancing Act", *Harvard Business Review*, July–August 2010, https://hbr.org/2010/07/the-globe-singapore-airlines-balancing-act.
72 www.lawnet.co.uk and www.lawnet.co.uk/membership-benefits/learning-development/.
73 Carnegie, n 11.
74 www.open.edu/openlearn/.
75 Zack Friedman, "Google says the best teams have these five things", *Forbes*, 28 January 2019, www.forbes.com/sites/zackfriedman/2019/01/28/google-says-the-best-teams-have-these-5-things/#45207b5f5a30.

76 Joseph Luft and Harrington Ingham, "The Johari window, a graphic model of interpersonal awareness", proceedings of the Western Training Laboratory in Group Development (University of California, Los Angeles 1955).

77 www.performanceleader.com/.

78 www.edwddebono.com/.

79 Jim Collins, *Good to Great* (Random House Business 2001).

80 Stephen R Covey, *Seven Habits of Highly Effective People* (Simon and Schuster; reprinted edition 2004).

81 www.djblearning.co.uk/.

82 The full SRA report, "Understanding implementation of our approach to continuing competence 2 July 2019", can be accessed at www.sra.org.uk/sra/how-we-work/reports/continuing-competence.

83 Diane Coutu, "The Anxiety of Learning", *Harvard Business Review*, March 2002, https://hbr.org/2002/03/the-anxiety-of-learning.

84 Carol S Dweck, *Mindset: The New Psychology of Success* (Ballantine Books 2007).

85 Nick Tasler, "Why 1 in 3 People Adapt to Change More Successfully", *Psychology Today*, 22 June 2016, www.psychologytoday.com/gb/blog/strategic-thinking/201606/why-1-in-3-people-adapt-change-more-successfully.

86 Cited in Tasler, n 85.

87 Chip Heath and Dan Heath, *Switch: How to Change when Change is Hard* (Random House 2011).

88 Campbell MacPherson, *The Change Catalyst: Secrets to Successful and Sustainable Business Change* (John Wiley & Sons 2017).

89 Hilary Scarlett, *Neuroscience for Organizational Change: An Evidence-Based Practical Guide to Managing Change* (Kogan Page 2019).

90 Kevin Ochsner, "The Formation of Habit", AmAreWay, 11 February 2011, www.amareway.org/holisticliving/02/the-formation-of-habit-kevin-ochsner/.

91 Jos Arets, Charles Jennings, Vivian Heijnen , "What is the 70:20:10 model?", Whitepaper: 70:20:10 into action 70:20:10 Institute, https://702010institute.com/702010-model/.

92 Generally attributed to Gordon Training International by employee Noel Burch in the 1970s.

93 Cited in Saul McLeod, "Kolb's Learning Styles and Experiential Learning Cycle, *Simply Psychology*, 2017 , www.simplypsychology.org/learning-kolb.html.

94 Peter Honey and Alan Mumford, *Manual of Learning Styles* (Peter Honey 1982).

95 Robert Bjork, "The Benefits of Interleaving Practice", 14 July 2012, https://youtu.be/l-1K61BallA; https://bjorklab.psych.ucla.edu/research/.

96 Hermann Ebbinghaus first described the learning curve in 1885 in the field of psychology of learning, although the term did not come into use until 1903.

97 Donald Hebb, *The Organization of Behavior. A Neuropsychological Theory* (Wiley 1949).

98 Cited in "Education Theory Made Practical – Volume 2, Part 3: Spaced Repetition Theory", International Clinician Educators, 23 April 2018, https://icenetblog.royalcollege.ca/2018/04/24/education-theory-made-practical-2-spaced-repetition-theory/.

99 Brenda Kelley Kim, "Is laziness hardwired in the brain?", Labroots, 25 September 2018, www.labroots.com/trending/neuroscience/12817/laziness-hardwired-brain.

100 For example, Tim Ferriss, *The 4-Hour Work Week: Escape the 9–5, Live Anywhere and Join the New Rich* (Vermillion 2011).

101 Richard Boyatzis, Melvin L Smith and Ellen Van Oosten, *Helping People Change: Coaching with Compassion for Lifelong Learning and Growth* (Harvard Business Review Press 2019).

102 Chartered Institute of Marketing, Professional Marketing Competencies 2016, www.cim.co.uk/media/4038/professional-marketing-competencies-2016-interactive.pdf.

103 Full details of all award winners can be accessed at www.mpfglobal.com/awards/awards-2020.aspx.

104 https://qdooz.com/.

105 Rob Cross, Reb Rebele and Adam Grant, "Collaborative Overload", *Harvard Business Review*, January–February 2016, https://hbr.org/2016/01/collaborative-overload.

106 Lewis Carroll, *Alice's Adventures in Wonderland* (Macmillan & Co 1865).

107 Ken Blanchard and Spencer Johnson, *The New One Minute Manager* (Harper 2015).

108 For further details on this, see Kim Tasso, "Strategy and scenario planning: Blowing the cobwebs off your mind workshop", 9 September 2012, https://kimtasso.com/strategy-and-scenario-planning-blowing-the-cobwebs-off-your-mind-workshop-with-allen-overy/.

109 Boyatzis, Smith and Van Oosten, n 101.

110 Edwin A Locke, "Towards a theory of task motivation and incentives", *Organizational Behavior and Human Performance*, May 1968, www.sciencedirect.com/science/article/abs/pii/0030507368900044.

111 Johann Hari, *Lost Connections: Uncovering the Real Causes of Depression – And the Unexpected Solutions* (Bloomsbury 2018).

112 Rock and Siegal, n 63.

113 Shana Lebowitz, "A psychologist told me how she successfully navigated her way through a dilemma we've all faced", *Business Insider*, 19 June 2016, www.businessinsider.com/gabriele-oettingen-woop-2016-6?r=US&IR=T.

114 Editor @CforST, "What is the API model?", Center for Sustainability Transformation, 15 December 2016, http://sustainabilitytransformation.com/what-is-the-api-method/.

115 World of Work Project, "The PVI Model: Perception, Visibility and Influence", https://worldofwork.io/2019/05/the-pvi-model-perception-visibility-and-influence/.
116 Daniel Priestley, *Key Person of Influence: The Five-Step Method to Become One of the Most Highly Valued and Highly Paid People in Your Industry* (Rethink Press 2014).
117 James D Murphy, *The Debrief Imperative: The Secret Tool That is Transforming Businesses the World Over* (Fastpencil 2011).
118 B882 (1992), Creative Management Course, Open University Open Business School.
119 Shane Scott, *Born Entrepreneurs, Born Leaders: How Your Genes Affect Your Work Life* (Oxford University Press 2010).
120 British Psychological Society, Neo Personality Inventory Test, 2003/2009, https://ptc.bps.org.uk/test-review/neo-personality-inventory.
121 The HBDI is a system to measure thinking preferences developed by William Herrmann while he led management education at a General Electric facility. His ideas have informed the Whole Brain® Thinking methodology at Herrmann; www.hbdi.com/online-reference-and-activity-guide/a/index.html.
122 https://kaicentre.com/.
123 Robert Epstein and Victoria Phan, "Which competencies are the most important for creative expression?" *Creativity Research Journal*, 2012, www.researchgate.net/publication/271753629_Which_Competencies_Are_Most_Important_for_Creative_Expression.
124 Nancy Kline, *Time to Think: Listening to Ignite the Human Mind* (Cassell 2002).
125 Arthur B Van Gundy, Jr, *Techniques of Structured Problem Solving* (Second edition) (Van Nostrand Reinhold 1988).
126 A good source of information on a variety of creativity techniques is Peter Cook, *Best Practice Creativity* (Gower Publishing 1998). See also Edward de Bono, *Six Thinking Hats* (Penguin Life 2016).
127 www.ideo.com/about.
128 www.bl.uk/people/albert-mehrabian.
129 Alex (Sandy) Pentland, "To Signal is Human", *American Scientist*, May–June 2010, www.americanscientist.org/article/to-signal-is-human.
130 Stephanie Perkin, *Lola and the Boy Next Door* (Usborne, 2014).
131 Amy Cuddy, "Your body language may shape who you are", TEDGlobal 2012, www.ted.com/talks/amy_cuddy_your_body_language_may_shape_who_you_are?utm_campaign=tedspread&utm_medium=referral&utm_source=tedcomshare.
132 Covey, n 80.
133 Jennifer Aaker, "Harnessing the Power of Stories", VMware Women's Leadership Innovation Lab, Stanford University, November 2019, https://womensleadership.stanford.edu/stories.
134 Saul McLeod, "Short Term Memory", *Simply Psychology*, 2009, www.simplypsychology.org/short-term-memory.html.
135 Christopher Booker, *The Seven Basic Plots: Why We Tell Stories* (Continuum 2005).
136 Ashley Dugger, "The Inverted Pyramid in Journalistic Writing", Study.com, 16 December 2015, http://study.com/academy/lesson/the-inverted-pyramid-in-journalistic-writing.html.
137 Kim Tasso, *Better Business Relationships: Insights from Psychology and Management for Working in a Digital World* (Bloomsbury 2019).
138 Leslie A Baxter Kristina M Scharp, "Dialectical Tensions in Relationships", *International Encyclopedia of Interpersonal Communication*, June 2015, https://onlinelibrary.wiley.com/doi/full/10.1002/9781118540190.wbeic017.
139 Jade Mazarin, "Knapp's Model of Interaction Stages", Study.com, https://study.com/academy/lesson/knapps-model-of-interaction-stages.html.
140 Dwayne D Gremler and Kevin P Gwinner, "Customer-Employee Rapport in Service Relationships", *Journal of Service Research*, August 2000, www.gremler.net/personal/research/2000_Rapport_JSR.pdf.
141 Tsedal Neeley, "How to Build Trust with Colleagues You Rarely See", *Harvard Business Review*, 29 January 2018, https://hbr.org/2018/01/how-to-build-trust-with-colleagues-you-rarely-see.
142 Jon Ingham Kogan, *The Social Organization: Developing Employee Connections and Relationships for Improved Business Performance* (Kogan Page 2017).
143 Daniel Goleman, "How Emotionally Intelligent Are You?", 21 April 2015, www.danielgoleman.info/daniel-goleman-how-emotionally-intelligent-are-you/.
144 Robert M Morgan and Shelby D Hunt, "The Commitment-Trust Theory of Relationship Marketing", *Journal of Marketing*, July 1994, www.jstor.org/stable/1252308?seq=1.
145 Alan S Dick and Kunal Basu, "Customer Loyalty: Toward an Integrated Conceptual Framework", *Journal of the Academy of Marketing Science*, March 1994, https://link.springer.com/article/10.1177/0092070394222001.
146 In 2003 Fred Reichheld, a partner at Bain & Company, created a new way of measuring how well an organisation treats the people whose lives it affects – how well it generates relationships worthy of loyalty. He called that metric the NPS. He shared the methodology so anyone could apply it. www.netpromotersystem.com/resources/trademarks-and-licensing/.
147 Michael Grinder, *The Elusive Obvious* (Michael Grinder & Associates 2007).
148 MindTools Content Team, "McClelland's Human Motivation Theory: Discovering What Drives Members of Your Team", www.mindtools.com/pages/article/human-motivation-theory.htm.

149 Linda Tickle-Degnen and Robert Rosenthal, "The Nature of Rapport and Its Non-verbal Correlates", *Psychological Inquiry* 1990 Issue 4, www.tandfonline.com/doi/abs/10.1207/s15327965pli0104_1.
150 Steve J Martin, Noah J Goldstein, Robert Cialdini, *The Small Big: Small Changes That Spark Big Influence* (Profile Books 2015).
151 Carnegie, n 11.
152 Diego Gambetta, *Trust: Making and Breaking Cooperative Relations* (University of Oxford 2000), www.researchgate.net/publication/255682316_Can_We_Trust_Trust_Diego_Gambetta.
153 Paul D Cousins and Euan Stanwix, "It's only a matter of confidence! A comparison of relationship management between Japanese and UK non-Japanese-owned vehicle manufacturers", *International Journal of Operations and Production Management* , Vol 21 No 9, 2001, www.research.manchester.ac.uk/portal/en/publications/its-only-a-matter-of-confidence-a-comparison-of-relationship-management-between-japanese-and-uk-nonjapaneseowned-vehicle-manufacturers(a0bfe554-76a5-4ed2-82e3-59741b82bcec).html.
154 Paul A Pavlou, "Institution-Based Trust in Interorganizational Exchange Relationships: The Role of Online B2B Marketplaces on Trust Formation" *Journal of Strategic Information Systems*, December 2002, www.sciencedirect.com/science/article/abs/pii/S0963868702000173.
155 David E Morrison and Julie Firmstone, "The Social Function of Trust and Implications for E-commerce", *International Journal of Advertising*, January 2000, www.researchgate.net/publication/268042305_The_social_function_of_trust_and_implications_for_E-commerce.
156 L Young and I Wilkinson, "The Role of Trust and Co-operation in Marketing Channels: A Preliminary Study", *European Journal of Marketing*, Vol 23 No 2 1989.
157 Trusted Advisor Associates, "Understanding the Trust Equation", https://trustedadvisor.com/why-trust-matters/understanding-trust/understanding-the-trust-equation.
158 Neeley, n 141.
159 Roy J Lewicki and Carolyn Wiethoff, "Trust, Trust Development, and Trust Repair" in Morton Deutsch and Peter T. Coleman (eds), *The Handbook of Conflict Resolution: Theory and Practice* (Jossey-Bas Publishers 2000), www.beyondintractability.org/artsum/lewicki-trust.
160 Christoph Engel, "Dictator Games: A Meta Study", *Experimental Economics*, November 2011, https://link.springer.com/article/10.1007/s10683-011-9283-7.
161 Stephen M R Covey, "How the Best Leaders Build Trust", Leadership Now, February 2009, www.leadershipnow.com/CoveyOnTrust.html.
162 Rise Performance, "How can a leader create a high trust environment?", https://riseperformancegroup.com/create-high-trust-environment/.
163 Hofstede Insights, "National Culture", https://hi.hofstede-insights.com/national-culture.
164 Fons Trompenaars and Charles Hampden-Turner, *Riding the Waves of Culture: Understanding Diversity in Global Business* (Nicholas Brealey Publishing 2012).
165 P Christopher Earley and Soon Ang, *Cultural Intelligence: Individual Interactions across Cultures* (Stanford University Press 2003).
166 William W Wilmot and Joyce L Hocker, *Interpersonal Conflict* (McGraw-Hill Higher Education 2005).
167 Julian Dahl, "WIN-WIN: The Learnings of Kurt Lewin and Morton Deutsch", Dignita Law, 28 April 2018, https://dignitalaw.wordpress.com/2012/04/28/win-win-the-learnings-of-kurt-lewin-and-morton-deutsch/.
168 Wilmot and Hocker, n 166.
169 Mind Tools Content Team, "French and Raven's Five Forms of Power: Understanding Where Power Comes From in the Workplace Mindtools", www.mindtools.com/pages/article/newLDR_56.htm.
170 Manage Train Learn, "Conflict Resolution: The Thomas-Kilmann Model", www.managetrainlearn.com/page/conflict-resolution-model.
171 Roger Fisher and William Ury, *Getting to Yes: Negotiating Agreement Without Giving In* (Penguin 1983).
172 Ali Terai, "Negotiation and deal making masterclass – what I learned at Harvard Law School", 27 December 2017, www.youtube.com/watch?v=5bAbKnzEipM.
173 Neil Denny, *Conversational Riffs: Creating Meaning Out of Conflict* (Eldamar Ltd 2010).
174 Center for Creative Leadership, "The Core Leadership Skills You Need in Every Role – The "Fundamental 4" Leadership Skills for Leaders" www.ccl.org/articles/leading-effectively-articles/fundamental-4-core-leadership-skills-for-every-career-stage/.
175 Nigel Clark, Ben Kent, Alastair Beddow and Adrian Furner, *Professional Services Leadership Handbook: How to Lead a Professional Services Firm in a New Age of Competitive Disruption* (Kogan Page 2017).
176 Ros Jay and Richard Templar, *Fast Thinking Manager's Manual* (Prentice Hall 2004).
177 John Whitmore, *Coaching for Performance: The Principles and Practice of Coaching and Leadership* (25th anniversary edition) (Nicholas Brealey Publishing 2017).
178 Mike Schultz, John E. Doerr and Neil Rackham, *Insight Selling: Surprising Research on What Sales Winners Do Differently* (John Wiley & Sons 2014).
179 Mary Morrissey, "The Power of Writing Down Your Goals and Dreams", Huffpost, 14 September 2016, www.huffpost.com/entry/the-power-of-writing-down_b_12002348.
180 Boyatzis, Smith and Van Oosten, n 68.

181 *Ibid.*
182 Kate Ludeman, "To Fill the Feedback Void" *Training & Development*, August 1995.
183 Courtney Seiter, "The Art and Science of Giving and Receiving Criticism at Work", Fast Company, 12 September 2014, www.fastcompany.com/3039412/the-art-science-to-giving-and-receiving-criticism-at-work.
184 Naomi I Eisenberger, "The Neural Bases of Social Pain: Evidence for Shared Representations with Physical Pain", *Psychosomatic Medicine*, February 2012, www.ncbi.nlm.nih.gov/pmc/articles/PMC3273616/.
185 Teresa Amabile, "The Progress Principle", TEDxAtlanta, 12 October 2011, https://youtu.be/XD6N8bsjOEE.
186 Blanchard and Johnson, n 107.
187 Kline, n 124.
188 Geoffrey James, "10 smart rules for giving negative feedback", Inc.com, 21 August 2012, www.inc.com/geoffrey-james/how-to-give-negative-feedback-10-rules.html.
189 Jim Trinka and Les Wallace, A Legacy of 21st Century Leadership: A Guide for Creating a Climate of Leadership Throughout Your Organization (iUniverse 2007).
190 Jack Zenger and Joseph Folkman, "Your employees want the negative feedback you hate to give", *Harvard Business Review*, 15 January 2014, https://hbr.org/2014/01/your-employees-want-the-negative-feedback-you-hate-to-give.
191 Elisabeth Kübler-Ross, *On Death and Dying* (Simon & Schuster/Touchstone 1969).
192 Management Study Guide, "Kurt Lewin's Change Management Model: The Planned Approach to Organizational Change", www.managementstudyguide.com/kurt-lewins-change-management-model.htm.
193 LexisNexis InterAction, *2019 Law Firm Marketing & Business Development Survey*, March 2020, www.interaction.com/2019-bd-survey-report/.
194 Keith Rollag, "Succeed in New Situations", *Harvard Business Review*, December 2015, https://hbr.org/2015/12/succeed-in-new-situations.
195 Kim Tasso, *Dynamic Practice Development: Selling Skills and Techniques for the Professions* (Thorogood 2003).
196 Kim Tasso, *Social Media in Business Development and Relationship Management: A Guide for Lawyers* (Globe Law and Business 2018).
197 Cited in Theodore Levill, "Marketing Myopia", *Harvard Business Review*, July–August 2004, https://hbr.org/2004/07/marketing-myopia.
198 Robert W Swaim, "Peter Drucker on Sales and Marketing", Process Excellence Network, 18 February 2013, www.processexcellencenetwork.com/innovation/columns/peter-drucker-on-sales-and-marketing.
199 Huthwaite International, "What is SPIN® Sellling?", www.huthwaiteinternational.com/business-performance-solutions/sales-training/about-spin/.
200 PACE, "PACE Programmes", https://thepacepartners.com/pace-programmes/.
201 Mike Schultz and John Doerr, *Insight Selling: Surprising Research on What Sales Winners Do Differently* (John Wiley & Sons 2014).
202 Gartner, "The New B2B Buying Journey", www.gartner.com/en/sales/insights/b2b-buying-journey.
203 For example, Robert Cialdini, *Influence: The Psychology of Persuasion* (Harper Business 2007).
204 For example, Thaler and Sunstein, n 66.
205 www.lawsociety.org.uk/law-careers/career-progression/soft-skills/.
206 ICAEW, "Soft Skills Development", www.icaew.com/membership/support-throughout-your-career/career-progression/soft-skills-development; and "Accountants Need Soft Skills", www.icaew.com/learning-and-development/job-essential-skills/employability-skills/which-skills-and-behaviours-do-employers-want-to-see/accountants-need-soft-skills.
207 Sage report, *The Practice of Now 2019: An Essential Report for Accountants*, www.sage.com/en-gb/blog/practice-of-now/.
208 PwC, "PwC's Whole Leadership Award", www.pwc.com/sg/en/careers/students/talent-programmes/whole-leadership-award.html.
209 ICAEW, "Developing Leadership in Practice (DLiP™), www.icaew.com/learning-and-development/academy/leadership-development-programmes/developing-leadership-in-practice.
210 RICS, "RICS Requirements and Competencies Guide", August 2018, www.rics.org/globalassets/rics-website/media/qualify/pathway-guides/pathway-guides-requirements-and-competencies-v1.3-oct-2018.pdf.
211 http://letg.org.uk/.
212 www.lawsociety.ie/Courses—Events/cpd/FinuasSkillnet/.
213 G Orme, n 34.

About the author

Kim Tasso
Managing director, RedStarKim Ltd
kim@kimtasso.com

Kim Tasso BA (Hons) DipM FCIM MCIJ MBPsS MBA is the managing director of RedStarKim Ltd. She is an independent management consultant and professional coach/trainer, specialising in the professional services sector, with over 30 years' experience.

After qualifying in psychology and working for several years in the technology sector, she worked for a number of leading professional service firms (Deloitte and Nabarro Nathanson (now part of CMS)) before starting her own business in January 1994.

She has since worked for more than 300 clients, including solicitors' firms, barristers' chambers, patent attorneys, accountancy practices, insolvency practitioners, actuaries, surveyors, marketing services agencies and management consultants.

She advises on and provides training and coaching in the strategic and operational aspects of management, change, marketing, business development, sales and client relationship management. She has published six books (on selling, media relations, growth strategies and business relationships) and hundreds of articles.

She has held various non-executive director positions in the property industry and is a trustee of a mental health charity.

About Globe Law and Business

Globe Law and Business was established in 2005. From the very beginning, we set out to create law books which are sufficiently high level to be of real use to the experienced professional, yet still accessible and easy to navigate. Most of our authors are drawn from Magic Circle and other top commercial firms, both in the United Kingdom and internationally.

Our titles are carefully produced, with the utmost attention paid to editorial, design and production processes. We hope this results in high-quality books which are easy to read, and a pleasure to own. All our new books are also available as ebooks, which are compatible with most desktop, laptop and tablet devices. We have recently expanded our portfolio to include a new range of journals and Special Reports, available both digitally and in hard copy format, and produced to the same high standards as our books.

We'd very much like to hear from you with your thoughts and ideas for improving what we offer. Please do feel free to email me at sian@globelawandbusiness.com with your views.

Sian O'Neill
Managing director
Globe Law and Business
www.globelawandbusiness.com